TELL ME A
HUNTIN' STORY

STEVE CHAPMAN
AND DON HICKS

HARVEST HOUSE PUBLISHERS

Cover Image © Brad Herndon; sharply_done, AVTG, drpnncpp, FRANKHILDEBRAND / iStock

Cover design by Bryce Williamson

Interior design by Chad Dougherty

TELL ME A HUNTIN' STORY
Copyright © 2017 Steve Chapman and Don Hicks
Published by Harvest House Publishers
Eugene, Oregon 97408
www.harvesthousepublishers.com

ISBN 978-0-7369-7069-3 (pbk.)
ISBN 978-0-7369-7070-9 (eBook)

Printed in the United States of America

17 18 19 20 21 22 23 24 25 26 / BP-CD / 10 9 8 7 6 5 4 3 2 1

From Don

I dedicate these writings to my wonderful wife, Doris. She's my partner, my best friend, and the love of my life. No other woman in the universe would endure my insane compulsion for waking up at ridiculously early hours, ransacking the pantry for edible goodies, and departing to brave the harsh elements just for a chance to engage in a battle of wits with some of nature's smartest critters.

From Steve

Sometimes when I'm sitting quietly in the woods, watching, waiting, and deeply enjoying where I am and what I'm blessed to be doing, gratitude wells up in me for the man who introduced me to the glorious world of hunting. I dedicate this book to the memory of my longtime friend and fellow West Virginia hunter, Kenneth Bledsoe.

Acknowledgments

From Don

I give special thanks to Steve Chapman, who encouraged me to transfer these stories from my heart to paper, to Teresa Jenkins and Patty Howell for their assistance in the writing process, and especially to those who have lived these stories with me. Thank you for letting me pass them on to others.

From Steve

My sincere thanks to Harvest House Publishers for providing Don and me the opportunity to encourage and inspire our fellow hunters through this collection of some of our favorite stories.

Contents

Preface

STEVE

I'll never forget meeting Don Hicks for the first time. He and his wife, Doris, traveled from midstate Indiana to attend a marriage conference Annie and I conducted at the Cove on the grounds of the Billy Graham Training Center in Asheville, North Carolina. During the first of four sessions, I mentioned my avid love of hunting, primarily for the sake of building a connection with my fellow outdoorsmen in the room.

After the session Don came to me with a big grin on his bearded face and announced that he, too, was a passionate hunter. Within seconds (literally!) we felt like longtime friends. Before we headed to lunch with the rest of the group, he said, "You should come to Indiana someday and hunt with me." He had no idea how seriously I would consider hunting with a resident of one of the best whitetail states in the nation. I said, "Can we leave right now?"

Eventually I did go to Indiana and chase deer with Don. I have a really nice eleven-point rack in my possession to prove it. In addition to providing the hunting opportunities, he was gracious enough to host Annie and me at a concert in his area. As a show of thanks for his friendship and hospitality, I prepared a very special gift to present to him during the event. It was a back scratcher—but not your run-of-the-mill, plastic, mass-produced type of back scratcher. It was handmade with great care at my workbench in our garage.

Weeks earlier, I tagged a very mature Tennessee gobbler. I cut off one of its legs just above the knee, and I wrapped the turkey's foot and claws around a golf ball and taped them into place. After about a month the claws hardened into the shape needed for creating my masterpiece. Then I stained an 18-inch-long, half-inch-thick wooden dowel with a beautiful walnut finish. Next, using a drill bit that matched the dowel width, I drilled a hole into the top of the knee joint of the wild turkey leg. It was artistry at its finest.

With leather strips and epoxy glue I attached the wild turkey leg to the wooden dowel, and the end result was, without question, the most unique, most effective, and ugliest back scratcher ever made. I couldn't wait to give it to Don in a public setting.

When the moment came for the presentation, I removed the turkey-claw back scratcher from a nicely wrapped cardboard tube to show the crowd, and I heard a corporate gasp. I looked across the auditorium, and every face had an expression that seemed to say, "I'm not sure what I'm seeing, but I'm so glad that thing isn't for me." But not Don. He was visibly excited and button-popping proud. You'd thought he'd won a Grammy for album of the year. His reaction to my hideous handmade turkey-foot masterpiece quadrupled his likeability factor in my mind.

That brief encounter with Don in North Carolina sparked a fellowship that has now spanned several years. While sitting side by side in deer stands and turkey blinds, we've talked (actually, whispered) for hours. We've laughed till we could hardly breathe, and we've even fought back a tear or two as we shared about the challenges of life...all while engaged in the thrill of the fair chase.

I'm thankful for our friendship, and not just because he lives in big-antler territory and is willing to share the monster bucks with me. I'm delighted because Don inspires me spiritually through his wealth of knowledge of God's Word and his deep devotion to prayer. I'm encouraged as a husband by his undying faithfulness to his lovely and supportive wife, Doris. His huge compassion for the people he pastors in the Indiana town of Campbellsburg challenges me to be more concerned for others. Don is the real deal, and I'm grateful to partner with him in telling you the stories we've put in this book. I hope you enjoy your time with us.

Introduction

STEVE

There's nothing like a good huntin' story! I've heard them at hunting camps from Michigan to Alabama to Tennessee, and around tables at wild-game dinner events in states like Pennsylvania, South Carolina, and Minnesota. I've been glued to them outside of tents at spike camps in the Montana mountains, around a bonfire at a camp in the Colorado Rockies, in a skiff while on the backcountry waters of Alaska, and many other places where I've gathered with hunters—and I've never, ever been bored while listening.

Not only do I enjoy hearing a good huntin' story, I like watching others as they tell them. At airport waiting gates, for example, I might see two fellows talking who are dressed in their travel camo on their way to or from a hunt. Their exaggerated hand motions, the awe in their facial expressions, their sympathetic head shaking, or their laughter are sure signs of a story being told. As I observe their body language, it's clear that the one telling the tale is thoroughly enjoying reliving it, and the one taking it all in is immersed in the thrill of living it for the first time.

Why are hunting stories so loved by those of us who hunt? There are at least three good reasons. One, we simply can't get enough of the adventure, the adrenalin rush, and the challenge that hunting provides. Sharing experiences with each other is as life-giving to our passion as air is to our lungs.

A second reason is that very often we hear a detail in a story that teaches us something we can apply to our next hunt. Perhaps we glean a new stalking tactic, a tip about archery or firearm shooting, a different way to set up a deer stand, or some other yet-to-be-discovered, skill-enhancing nugget.

Third, there's a very important benefit that can be gained from a hunting story. It's one that my friend Don and I value immensely and long for our fellow outdoorsmen and women to appreciate, and that is that heart-changing insights are so often tucked away in stories about hunters and hunting.

Don and I thank you for choosing to walk with us down the trail of adventure that weaves from his voice to mine in these pages. As you participate in this "story swap," we hope you'll not only enjoy the hunting action but also find something meaningful for your life—something that will build up your character, inspire confidence in our Creator, stimulate your gratitude for your many blessings, and even improve your relationships with those you love. If any of these things happen, it will have been worth all the effort we made to write this book, which carries as its title the words we love to say...

Tell me a huntin' story!

1

Escape Route

DON

I won't forget the morning I watched a deer as it meandered through the woods toward me from my left. Then, for just a moment, I looked to my right toward a suspicious sound to make sure I didn't have a sneaker coming in from the opposite direction. When I turned my eyes back to the approaching deer I discovered that he had vanished...gone, never to be seen again. It was as though he was strangely, miraculously transported away from the danger of my presence. To try to explain how the deer mysteriously eluded the sharp razors on my arrow is as futile as attempting to give a logical explanation for another escape from deadly danger, but not by a deer. In this case, it was a hunter.

Lloyd Jones is as skilled at sneaking through the woods as any of the amazingly stealthy deer I've seen in my day, and there's a reason for it. Hunting is his passion, his therapy, so he does it often. Next to loving God and his family, there's nothing he likes to do more than load the bed of his pickup with his tree stand, his bow, and a pack filled with gear and food, and tell the world good-bye for a while as he heads to his favorite hunting place. It's what he was doing on an unusually hot and very dry morning in October.

Knowing that walking on the crunchy leaves could make him sound like a herd of cattle stampeding through a fresh box of corn-flakes, he wanted an extra-early entry into the woods, so he started driving well before sunrise to the farm he'd hunt. He was sure he wouldn't be heard by any of the deer that would arrive later that morning after a night of munching corn nubbins in the farm bottoms.

Lloyd attached his climber to a tree. Then he removed his sweat-soaked clothing, stuffed it in a plastic bag, dressed in his dry camo, and climbed to about twenty feet. With the long, thin rope attached to his bow that was still on the ground, he pulled it up, put an arrow on the string and settled in for the hunt.

By eight o'clock the bright beams of the morning sun filtered through the branches and began to raise the temperature. The wind that blew through the remaining dehydrated autumn leaves brought a welcome cooling to his face. He smiled at the thought that for the rest of the day he had nothing better to do than enjoy watching the woods.

A few moments later, Lloyd caught the sound of something scurrying up the hill toward his stand. Within another few seconds he saw a foursome of deer—three ladies and a massive mound of macho buckskin. As they moved quickly toward him, he noticed they seemed unusually restless and confused. He assumed a dog or maybe a coyote had them on the run. Whatever it was, he was happy for the action.

Lloyd tried to calm himself. The excitement had brought a nervous shake to his hands. *Just be patient. They don't have a clue I'm here, so just relax, stand up, and get ready. That buck is a taker.*

When the small herd got within forty yards, they slowed their pace for a moment but didn't stop. Lloyd was on his feet with his string release attached. Without being seen, he came to full draw and put his sight pin just forward of the front shoulder of the buck to accommodate for a broadside moving shot at about twenty yards. Then the unthinkable happened.

As he held at full draw, he got a whiff of an all too familiar smell. Having been a member of the local volunteer fire department for many years, he recognized it immediately—smoke! Not just the front-yard, leaf-burning variety, but the heavy, dense, dangerous smoke of a forest fire.

"No! Not now! Not today!"

The source of the smoke seemed to be close, so he quickly relaxed his string, quivered his arrow, gathered his gear, attached his bow to the rope, and lowered it to the ground. He was oblivious to the presence of the keeper buck as it passed directly under his stand.

Panic gripped him when he looked southward and saw a wall of smoke heading directly toward him. He couldn't yet see the flames, but he knew they were there and moving his way at freight-train speed.

With his bow now lying in the leaves, he loosened his safety harness and scurried down the tree. As soon as his feet hit the ground, he knew he was in serious trouble. Burning leaves were now blowing past him as he stood at the base of the trunk.

He looked in the direction he had entered earlier that morning and saw embers swirling like snowflakes on fire. It would be impossible to follow the same trail out. Flames raced across the dry forest floor and began to surround him. The wind, which earlier had been a friend in the morning heat, was now a forceful enemy as it pushed the flames along, forming a burning trap around him. Lloyd frantically searched his mind for a lifesaving plan. *What do I do?*

Being spiritually minded, he immediately did what any God-fearing man would do in a time of crisis. Closing his eyes and forcing himself to ignore his panic, he prayed a prayer that started with questions.

"Lord, what will the kids do? What will my wife do? Lord, I don't deserve any of the great things You've done for me, but if You don't come now, it's over for me. Please, Lord, come. Help me!"

It's amazing how certain thoughts can come to mind when danger looms. In Lloyd's case, his thoughts went to the Bible story of three Hebrew men who were thrown in a furnace. He thought of how the evil men who threw them in had been burned by the very blaze they started. But thanks to a fourth man who showed up in the fire with them, they walked out unharmed. No charred clothing. No scorched hair. No fried skin. Their clothes didn't even smell like smoke.

Lloyd continued to call out to God. "Lord, what You did for those Hebrew children, You can do for me. If it's just me in this burning forest, I'm done. But if You come, You can get me out. Come, Lord Jesus."

The prayer was the last thing he remembered.

When he awoke, he saw a nurse standing beside him with a needle in her hand. His eyes widened as he said, "Hey, I don't like needles."

The nurse, happy to see that he was finally awake and able to speak, replied, "Sir, this is one needle you should be thankful for. You could easily have died in that fire."

"Who got me outta there?" he asked.

"Got you out? I have no idea. All I know is that you were found lying by the edge of the road beside your vehicle. You must have found an escape route out of those woods, and fast! Someone said there's nothing left out there but charred timber and some hot patches. I heard they are yet to get the fire under control."

"The edge of the road? What?" Lloyd couldn't hide his bewilderment. "The last thing I remember is standing a few feet from my tree stand."

"Well, you got out somehow." The nurse smiled as she withdrew the needle from her patient's arm. "Maybe you have a great guardian angel. Assuming you do, if I were you I'd send him a thank-you card."

After a short stay in the hospital, Lloyd was released with instructions to recuperate at home for a few days. As he did, a "burning" question kept coming to his mind. *How did I get out of that inferno and back to my truck?* He wasn't the only one who wondered about it.

Those who heard about his near-death experience had different opinions about how he escaped. Some said it was just the product of the human survival instinct. Some credited adrenalin—that mysterious bodily substance that can take control in a time of shock and allow a human to do unexplainable things, like lift a car off of an accident victim or dig their way out of an avalanche. Others simply attributed his survival to luck or fate. Lloyd, however, came to a different conclusion.

After trying to figure it out and coming up with no answer for how he ended up next to his truck at the side of the road, he was convinced that God had come to the scene. From then on when someone asked him about it, he didn't hesitate to say it was a miracle. Whether through a man or an angel, somehow God showed up.

When Lloyd finally felt well enough to leave the house and make a short run to the store, he went to his driveway and started to climb in the cab of his truck. As he did, he happened to glance back at the bed. There, folded and placed exactly where he would have laid it, was his portable tree stand. No bow, quiver, or rope he used for a drop-line—just his stand.

In telling the story to me, he said something I have never forgotten. Tears came and his hands seemed to tremble a bit as he said, "The Bible says, 'Do not neglect to show hospitality to strangers, for thereby some have entertained angels unawares'" (Hebrews 13:2 ESV). We both smiled. I knew what he meant.

I still wonder…after the fire dissipated, did someone find the steel frame of a tree stand attached to a charred, downed tree and know that it belonged to Lloyd? Did someone find his address where he had written it on the bottom of the seat and deliver it without a word? Or did Lloyd instinctively lower it to the ground, disconnect it from the tree, strap it to his back, and carry it out of the woods with him as he crawled out on his hands and knees? It remains a mystery.

Like Lloyd, I suppose I'll never know exactly how his escape happened until I get to heaven and hear God's version of the story. For now, all I know is that in the face of grave danger, he was somehow delivered to safety. In his case, a portion of 1 Corinthians 10:13 really can apply. It says, "God is faithful…he will also provide the way of escape" (ESV). It's a truth that should encourage anyone who may feel trapped in some way. It might not be a forest fire that threatens, but perhaps it's a fast-moving blaze of sickness or the deadly flames of discontent, worry, fear, disappointment, or any other kind of fire that can rush in and destroy peace in the soul. I, for one, never want to forget that God is fully able to make a way of escape for me when there seems to be no way—just as He did for Lloyd in the fiery woods.

2

The Discovery

STEVE

I have a friend in my Tennessee neck of the woods that I hunt with often. Unlike many guys I know whose love for hunting started early in their lives, his came later. Here's how it happened.

Annie and I were about halfway through the six-week process of recording a CD of songs, and I was at the studio doing some of my vocal overdubs. When the session ended, I gathered up my lyric sheets, slid them into my shoulder bag, and headed to my truck. The producer, Lindsey, walked with me. He was at the driver's door when I opened it and put my stuff in the passenger seat. We chatted about the schedule for the next session, and I noticed he looked around me at the floorboard. Then he asked a question.

"You shoot guns?"

Another musician had introduced Annie and me to Lindsey only a few months prior when we were searching for a producer. For that reason he didn't know me all that well—and I didn't know him enough to know whether he was about to confront me about firearms. I answered a little cautiously.

"Uh…yes I do."

"What kind of pistol is that under your seat?"

I reached in the truck and retrieved the gun in its leather holster.

"This is a nine-mil Smith & Wesson police issue…bought it used at a store in south Nashville. It's there if I need it for self-defense, and I pray I never do. I have other guns, mostly rifles I use for hunting."

I went ahead and brought up the fact that I was a hunter just to get things out in the open. I was relieved to hear his response to my confession.

"Hmm…I've always wondered what hunting is like. Never done it."

I liked this new producer—and it wasn't just because he didn't attack me with an anti-hunting rant. While I was very grateful for that, there was more to appreciate about him. He had an easygoing presence in the studio and was highly skilled in the art. Even more important to Annie and me was Lindsey's obvious dedication to his wife and their two children. He had paid a ton of money to turn his garage into a recording studio so he could avoid being excessively absent from home.

Because he had won my favor with his professionalism, his personality, his family-first attitude, and his curiosity about hunting, I felt safe saying, "Well, I wouldn't mind at all taking you hunting someday. I can set you up with whatever gear you need. We look about the same size, so I can deck you out in camo, and you can use one of my guns. All you need is a license."

Lindsey's eyes lit up as he said, "Well, I may just take you up on that offer."

By the time October came in Tennessee, our recording was finished. (I always try to have the production done before hunting season starts. Mama didn't raise no fool!) The only thing left to do was travel to concerts on the weekends and hunt during the week as much as possible. I hunted through archery deer season, and when gun season arrived, I remembered Lindsey's interest in going to the woods. I gave him a call, and we made plans for an early morning trek to a deer stand together.

Nearly all of the longtime hunters I know will agree that there's hardly anything more enjoyable and satisfying than to take someone deer hunting who has never been. To see their eyes widen when a doe or buck comes in close enough to see the whiskers on their nose is more valuable than a gold record. When the newbie's breathing gets shallow and quick and their hands shake as they try to control their weapon, we know that more than likely they've been hooked deep. Lindsey was no exception.

Our first outing yielded only a close encounter with no shots fired, but I could tell by the way he profusely thanked me for the experience as we headed to my truck that my new friend was leaving the woods that day as more than a record producer. Now he was also a hunter. How right I was. And what a fast learner!

It had been a long time since I'd seen someone catch on so quickly to the necessity of keeping movement to an absolute minimum when on a deer stand. He sat like a statue that first day and moved even less than I did. When I spoke in a whisper, he answered with a whisper. It was as though he instinctively knew that hunting required some adjustments to our normal behavior.

I especially appreciated Lindsey's approach to handling a gun. I was grateful for how careful he was with my .270 when he fired a few rounds to get familiar with it. His "take no chances" attitude made me feel much safer, and I was sure it meant everything to his wife, Susan.

As it turned out, Lindsey and I made several trips to the woods that first rifle season of our friendship. With each hunt he got better and better at it. What a delight it was to have someone in close proximity who felt as much passion for the adventure as I did. In fact, he was so excited about hunting that within a few months he picked up a trio of guns for his arsenal (a .270 rifle, a 12-gauge shotgun, and a .50 caliber muzzleloader). I was so thrilled about his newfound interest that I added to his weaponry by passing along an extra compound bow that a manufacturer had given me.

The good news is that since Lindsey started hunting, his freezer has been consistently stocked with wild game, including deer, turkey, elk, and rabbit. The wholesome, lean, and tasty meat is a welcome byproduct of the various hunting seasons and trips he and I have enjoyed. Susan, who is a master cook and successful blogger about all things culinary, loves to get a call from the man she affectionately refers to as "Big Bison" with the news that shots were fired and he's bringin' home a "Boom & Cookit" trophy for the grill.

Sometimes I've thought about what an interesting thing it was that Lindsey, at nearly midlife, discovered a passion he didn't know was in him. It reminds me of a recurring dream that both Annie and I have had. In our dream we are in the house we've lived in for years, and one day we open a door to a room that we didn't know existed. The feeling in the dream is overwhelming as we walk into the yet-to-be-enjoyed space. The thrill is so real and so exciting that waking up is a huge letdown!

We're not psychologists, but our guess is that our dream is a natural response to the way we look at life—with an expectancy of discovery. We're always ready for a new adventure, and we're both happy to say we've found some "new rooms." For example, about three-quarters of the way through the 1990s, in my midforties, I discovered I liked to write more than just song lyrics. It happened when I was sitting with a group of hunters around a fire in a deer camp in Nebraska, and suddenly I got the idea for a book of hunting stories. I never dreamed that these many years later I'd still be chronicling my adventures.

More recently, Annie discovered a new room in her house. She had no clue how much she would enjoy sewing until the day her friend Laura came to visit and brought her a homemade item called a tea cozy. Something about the cozy captured Annie's imagination, and with Laura's tutorship, she started making unique, thermal-lined, eye-catching cloth covers for teapots that keep the water hotter for a longer time. Today she's busy making them as gifts for friends and family, and much to her surprise and delight, Annie's Tea Cozies are carried by a nationally known tearoom-restaurant in our area. "Who'd a thunk it?" as they say.

Our daughter, too, has discovered a room in her life-house she didn't know she had. One frigid January day as her three girls were doing their homeschool work, Heidi picked up an artist's brush and tried her hand at painting. What an amazing find she made in her midthirties! Her canvases grace the walls of our home and several others in the middle-Tennessee area, and the number of commissions for her work is growing.

Sometimes when standing by my tailgate before dawn, waiting for Lindsey to arrive at a farm where we'll hunt together, my thoughts go back to that moment when we walked out to my truck outside his home studio. When my door opened and he asked about my pistol, it's as though he suddenly looked into a room he didn't know was in his soul. What a discovery it was.

I could be wrong, but I have a feeling that in every life there is a beautiful and exciting room yet to be found. Maybe it's a hidden talent, a surprising new interest, or an untapped wellspring of compassion. Who knows? Well, Jesus does. He's the One who said, "In My Father's house are many mansions; if it were not so, I would have told you. I go to prepare a place for you" (John 14:2).

Think about it—a house with many mansions in it! That sounds like an exciting place to live. If God's house in heaven has awesome rooms waiting for discovery, why not ours while here on earth? After all, we're made in His image!

> Eye has not seen, nor ear heard,
> Nor have entered into the heart of man
> The things which God has prepared for those who love
>   Him (1 Corinthians 2:9).

3
Waiting with a True Friend

DON

Of all the friends who've gone with me to a deer stand, there's one who has helped me find success more than any other, and I think you'll be surprised to know that this friend is not a hunter.

One of the most amazing traits I have acquired from my wanderings in the woods near my home is that after many years, I can know with extreme accuracy exactly when and where my quarry will appear—even from which direction. This special gift has allowed me to sleep in a little longer, lessen my scouting time, and foreknow and practice the necessary body position for flinging an arrow or firing a musket ball.

And if you believe all that, you'll probably also believe I can walk on water, fly like an eagle, and chase down a deer in an open field.

The truth is, if I have learned anything over a lifetime of chasing fur and feather in the wild, it is that their ways are not my ways, nor are their thoughts my thoughts. Still, I always have a plan. What I know about chasing critters comes from years of woodland presence and preparation for my time in their world. I do things like lock, load, and fire my muzzleloader at my homemade gun range until I can consistently put a 250-grain lead bullet into a two-inch circle at 100 yards. For bow season, I practice pulling my compound string until my biceps feel as hard as the steel in the broadheads that tip my arrows. In addition, I spend a lot of time mentally planning an approach pattern and calculating wind direction so I can sneak into my well-thought-out hiding place. I work at it until I'm as sure as I can be that I've done all I can to be the victor in the man-versus-beast contest in the great outdoor coliseum.

The hours of practice, planning, packing, and picking just the right spot to set up are so exciting for me that by the time the morning comes to put all my prep to the test, my emotions are soaring. I'm so pumped that I nearly run to my stand. It's not uncommon for me to be there an hour before sunrise.

But then, after I've taken my seat, quietly removed the things I need from my pack and placed them within easy reach (binoculars, thermos, reloads, snacks, calls, and so on), and finally stopped moving, I discover that I have once again forgotten to prepare for one thing—the long wait.

I have to wait till there's enough daylight to shoot, and sometimes I have to wait for the sun to melt the frost off the field so the local herd wants to browse in it. I might have to wait till a dense fog lifts off the meadow. And then I have to wait on the deer to move through—if they do.

Waiting, especially if it requires hours for a critter to come into harvesting range, has a way of messing with important things like concentration, determination, and emotional stamina. Too much waiting can even make inactive muscles turn as stubborn as a cantankerous old mule.

One way I've tried to make the wait more enjoyable is to have food on hand. I carry corn nuts, caramels, and crunchy breakfast grains in just about every pocket and secret cranny of my camouflaged outerwear as well as in my daypack. I like the snacks not just because they taste good but also because they provide a pleasant diversion.

During one long morning vigil, I had eaten everything I had brought, and after a while I became desperate for something else to help me bide the time. I checked my backpack again for just a morsel, and I can't describe how happy I was when I discovered a bar of candy in the bottom of one of the side pockets. I didn't remember including it in my mix of treats that day, but I was so glad to find it.

Before I ripped into it, I decided to look on the wrapper to see if there was a "best if used by" date on it. When I saw the year that was stamped on the slick, orange paper, I realized it had been there since the last day of the previous season. I had to make a decision between easing the pain of waiting by eating it (and risking a hunt-stopping case of botulism) or leaving it unopened. It wasn't easy to do, but I put the expired treat in a ziplock that was already full of empty wrappers and an apple core, and then I went back to waiting.

I've used other things to help me deal with the waiting, including a good book and a small Bible. At times I've even tried writing poetry using the pad and pen that are always with me. But try as I may by using these tactics, ultimately I've found that only one thing helps me endure the grind of waiting—patience!

Patience is a true friend. He (a masculine reference because it's like having a hunting buddy with me) is willing to sit with me the entire time I'm out there waiting. He doesn't scold me when I get antsy and start gorging, shaking my leg, biting my nails, sighing deeply, or complaining that my stand seat is starting to feel as hard as a brick.

Instead of making me feel defeated, patience gently reminds me that the wait is an invaluable part of the hunt. It's also a perfect opportunity to ponder some pressing matters. *What am I going to get my sweetie for our anniversary? How can I tell her about the new crossbow I have my eye on?* Or more important, *What can I say to encourage a friend who just found out he has to have surgery?*

Patience also reminds me that when I wait, God can whisper to me through His written Word. He tenderly helps me remember that the Book of books is in my backpack and that waiting provides a great opportunity to take it out and hear what nugget of wisdom the Holy Spirit might impart as I listen through the pages.

Patience is also kind enough to suggest that waiting on a deer stand is a great time to pray. There are plenty of folks who could use an uplift in prayer, like my ailing friend whom I need to call. Then there's my beloved wife, our children and grandchildren, the members of the congregation I shepherd, our spiritually ill nation, and our leaders, who could definitely use some prayer while I wait.

Patience also doesn't judge me when I complain that I'm halfway through my fourth hour of waiting without a single sighting. He just sits quietly and smiles like a good friend. But he does have something to say when I finally see that huge set of antlers in the distance swaying side to side as the four-hooved owner carries it slowly toward me. Patience waits until after my arrow is dripping with lung blood to say, *See, this is what can happen when you let me come along! Now, stop shaking and prepare to do something redeemable, like thanking God for success. You still have to wait about thirty minutes before you dismount and go find the fruit of your labor.*

I want to be more like my friend patience, not only in the woods but also in the rest of life, especially as I wait for the Lord of all creation to show up—Christ Jesus. What would my friend suggest as I tarry?

He'd say, "Be patient, brethren, until the coming of the Lord" (James 5:7).

And so I will.

4

Communication Fail

STEVE

A couple of friends, Dan and Stan, couldn't resist an opportunity to join a few other hunters in a western state for their first elk hunt together. One memory of the trip is a standout, and it makes a point worth remembering.

Stan had been to the big mountains before and was familiar with the gear they'd need to take. Dan was new to the process, and he had a thousand questions about the adventure. He constantly emailed his buddy to get advice about everything from filling out the application for his tag to how to get physically ready for the thin air in the 8000-foot altitude where they'd be hunting. Stan didn't mind answering every inquiry. Getting ready to go was a huge part of the fun.

A plethora of items made their lists, but one was considered by both men to be of utmost importance. Knowing they'd be hunting in the backcountry wilderness of one of the state's largest national forests, and hearing that it was possible that they'd be separated by half a mile or more of dense and unfamiliar terrain, they wholeheartedly agreed that they would definitely need to take a good pair of walkie-talkies.

Dan's radios were the better of their sets. They'd use them during the hunt, but just in case of a malfunction, Stan took his set as well. Each of them carried plenty of extra AA batteries for peace of mind.

The two friends were like little boys when their plane flew between two snowcapped peaks in the Rocky Mountains and landed. Dan's eyes were wider than fried turkey eggs as he scanned the territory, which was totally unlike the mid-Southern state he called home. The peaks that towered above the little town where they spent the night were just as awesome as Stan had said they were.

The next morning the other hunters picked up Dan and Stan at their hotel, and by early afternoon the group was unloading gear from their pickup trucks, rolling four-wheelers off their trailers, and setting up camp. Dan and Stan spent the evening poring over topographical maps provided by the resident hunters, choosing which part of the wilderness they'd venture into, and getting a tutorial on the borrowed four-wheeler they'd be using. With the season starting at daybreak the next morning, it wasn't easy for everyone to fall asleep, but near midnight the strategizing finally ended and the snoring began.

The five o'clock wake-up call made for a short night, but Dan and Stan shot out of their sleeping bags like jacks out of a box. After some cereal, a cinnamon roll, some coffee, and a quick powwow with the other hunters, the two mounted their gas-powered stallion and headed out into the dark.

The trail they were to follow took some twists and turns up the mountain and across some creeks that made for a challenging trip, but the thirty-minute ride ended safely at the parking spot marked on the map they carried. The area was public land—open to other hunters—so as Dan and Stan put their packs and rifles over their shoulders, Stan had a suggestion regarding their usage of the walkie-talkies.

"If there are other hunters on this mountain, I assume they'll have radios too, and they may be on our channel. If we see an elk after we split up, it might be better to have some sort of code words to keep someone from hearing what we say and moving in on us."

Dan buckled the front straps of his backpack around his chest. "You're right. Any ideas?"

"How about this. If I see an elk that's moving toward you, I'll buzz you and say, 'I just talked to Andrea on the cell.' And if you see an elk moving in my direction, you can call me and say, 'I just talked to Deloris on the cell.'"

"That sounds good. I hope one of us makes that call."

Forty-five minutes later, the sky began to lighten and reveal the stunning scenery around them. The two friends were in awe as they found the meadow they were looking for and split up. They agreed to hunt the entire day if needed, and if one fired shots, the other would come quickly to help.

Dan settled in against an aspen that allowed a good backrest and an excellent easterly view of the three-acre meadow surrounded by tall, dark-blue spruce trees. Stan ascended to a rocky outcrop that was perfect for monitoring a long flat that was at least forty yards wide. Four hours passed without a sighting, but the two friends were enjoying the sit so much, it felt like four minutes.

The first day of elk rifle season happened to fall on Stan's wife's birthday, but it was two o'clock in the afternoon before he remembered. He dug for his phone and was relieved to see that because of the altitude, he had enough signal to call home. He talked a few minutes with Andrea, wished her a happy birthday, and assured her that he was safe.

Thankful to have avoided the blunder of forgetting such an important day, Stan thought Dan would enjoy a report about his brush with spousal disaster. He pushed the call button on his radio and waited. Finally, he heard Dan say, "What's up?"

"Well, I just talked to Andrea on my cell."

There was total silence on the other end that lasted a few seconds. Before Stan could tell Dan about remembering his wife's birthday, Dan spoke—but his voice was obviously shaken.

"Okay! Talk soon."

"What? Dan? Hello?"

Stan buzzed Dan again. Several seconds passed before he answered.

Dan sounded nervous as he said, "So you talked to Andrea?"

"I did. I almost forgot to call her…"

Before Stan could explain more about the call, Dan said, "Okay, I understand," and went silent.

Stan was puzzled by his friend's response and put his radio in his pocket to think about it. He had no idea what he had just done. He didn't know that at the end of the meadow, his buddy was a ball of nerves as he intensely watched for an approaching elk.

Fifteen minutes went by, and Stan's radio buzzed.

"Hey, man, I thought you talked to Andrea on the cell. Nothing is happening over here."

Stan wondered what his buddy's report meant and asked, "Do you mean your cell's not working? Mine worked fine."

"What?" Dan was obviously bewildered.

"Did you try calling Deloris?"

"No way. I'm not about to do that. I'm still looking for something to walk in!"

Stan took his cap off and scratched his head, completely confused by the conversation. Then he tried again to make some sense out of the exchange by giving his friend a quick summary of his call home.

"Uh…today is Andrea's birthday, I almost forgot to call her, but I got through, and she was happy to hear from me. I avoided a husband blunder today."

Once again, Dan didn't say a word for a few moments. Then he broke the news to Stan.

"Dude, do you know I've been dealing with heart palpitations over here?"

"Say what?"

"Oh yeah. When you buzzed me a while ago and said you talked to Andrea on your cell, I went into hyper search mode. I've been fighting the shakes and have nearly left the imprint of my fingers on the stock of my gun."

Suddenly, it dawned on Stan what had happened. He realized he totally forgot about the code words they had agreed to use if he spotted an elk moving toward his friend. It explained Dan's nervous voice over his radio. It was time to apologize.

"Oh, man. I'm so sorry. I had a brain freeze. I had no idea I sent you into a nervous dither. I can only imagine what someone is thinking if they're hearing us talk. They'll think we're nuts."

"Only one of us is nuts!"

Stan pushed his talk button and couldn't hide the laughter in his voice as he spoke.

"I'm imagining the expression on your face when I called a while ago. I'd give a hundred bucks to see it."

Stan was happy to hear nothing but laughter when he heard Dan respond. He had no doubt the two of them were sharing a comical moment they would never forget.

The day ended without a sighting, and as the two friends met up at the center of the meadow to walk back to the four-wheeler together, they laughed some more about the communication fail they had enjoyed that day. When they arrived back at camp and gathered with the rest of the hunters for dinner, they took turns telling their version of what had happened on the mountain. They were both surprised when one of the resident hunters dropped a bomb on their story.

"You two obviously didn't know that using radios while elk hunting in this national forest is illegal. Just be glad there wasn't a guy in a uniform waiting for you at your four-wheeler this evening."

Dan and Stan looked at each other as the color drained from their faces. Dan said, "Well, good buddy, we're guilty of unintentional sin. Thank God there's grace for that too. I'm just glad that we're not packing up to leave, that we still have our rifles, and that we don't have a fine to pay. I guess we'll be turning our radios off for the rest of the week."

Stan agreed and then asked his buddy, "But if I talk to Andrea on my cell, should I call you and let you know?"

Dan shook his head and said, "Don't do it. I'm not sure my heart could take it!"

5

Opening-Day Wound

DON

Let me take you back to a previous season and describe one of the widest swings of emotion I've ever known. I'll start the morning before opening day of deer season here in Indiana.

It's almost a new year, but not the way most folks would count. It's not one 365-day journey of the earth around the sun that makes my calendar year. Instead, it's my hunting schedule. It's how I mark the passage of time. My mind goes season to season. It's Friday, and the new year starts in less than twenty-four hours!

At work, the morning passes like a slug on crutches, and the afternoon moves like cold molasses. I hang on and think about tomorrow.

Saturday is usually a honey-do day, but not this week. I have been graciously excused from that routine by my understanding bride. Instead, tomorrow is my long awaited annual "leap day"—I leap out of bed and run to the woods.

Five o'clock finally arrives at my workplace. I quickstep to the parking lot while digging in my pocket for my truck key, start the motor and race it twice for a quick warm-up, drop it in gear, and roar away toward hunting greatness. The one I'm after this year just might put me in the record books.

I wolf down an early dinner and skip the Friday night movie. Instead, the time is reserved for making sure each and every item is in its place, all areas covered. No room for mistakes now, for my survival and success in the big woods is at stake. My backpack is a matter of life and death—life for me and the end of the line for my quarry.

If sleep would just come, I know morning would arrive in a millisecond. This happens every fall. The almanac must be wrong—the night before deer season is surely the longest of the year.

I set the alarm, turn out the light, and see that massive rack in my fantasies once more. It's a picture of perfection penciled in the sketchbook of my mind. It's almost time to go find it.

Sleeping Beauty has her day planned as well—a trip to the mall, lunch with a few of her favorite gals, and an afternoon nap. She'll enjoy her day. Man, is life good or what! It will be another dream day at my place.

The alarm screams. Any other day it would completely shatter my nerves as it blasts like a tornado alert. But not this day. The sound is music to my ears!

Leaping out of my slumber like a kid on Christmas morning, trying not to awaken Beauty, I slip down the stairway, quiet as a mouse.

Making that predawn pot of coffee, I measure enough for one

cup that I'll drink before leaving the house and five to eight more cups that will wait quietly and steamy hot inside my Stanley thermos. Two extra scoops of those Columbian ground beans should do it. As I'm finishing that first cup, the radio assures me the weather will be perfect—cold and dry. Let's do it!

The clothes and boots I laid out yesterday evening wait just inside the back door. My exit strategy is in place. I know the routine well. I could do it in the dark: long johns, wool socks, my outerwear. It's a well-honed, step-by-step plan of dress that will keep me comfortable no matter what.

My weapon of choice stands silently at attention against the wall like a soldier waiting for orders.

Convinced that the worst day hunting is better than the best day working, I begin my joyful journey. I maneuver my way along the stone walkway that leads away from the lights of my home, and at the end of it I slide the flashlight switch to the on position. The beam guides me down the unlit trail to the beginning of another year of delight.

It's amazing how the body never tires while walking through predawn maze of cumbersome brush, over downed tree limbs, and across holes in the night floor that can capture a foot like a bear trap. I willingly take the risk.

It may take an extra moment in the blackness of early morning, but I will find my stand. I was close on my first try but missed. I know it's there, waiting to perch my body twenty feet above the forest floor. Aha, there it is. I climb in and become the king of the woodlands.

I planned on being early, but as I switch on my flashlight to look at my watch and make sure I'm on time, I realize I'm way ahead of schedule. An hour till dawn—must be because I left the house an hour early!

Sitting in the still of the final hour of night, I feel as if I'm a million miles from anywhere. I can hear sounds. I'm so pumped about hunting again that I imagine lions, tigers, elephants, and grizzlies. But in reality, I'm hearing coons and other smaller tree dwellers. An owl speaks, followed by a cardinal's wake-up song, and finally the rustling of fresh-fallen leaves as a waking squirrel jolts my morning.

Finally, like a slow-motion burst of lightning, the rising eastern sun appears behind me and wraps around the trunk of the tree I'm sitting in. It warms only my shoulders. Those blinding rays won't hit me in the face this morning. It's part of my plan. I will allow nature's spotlight to assist me in my quest for greatness. The solar smile will be in the deer's eyes, hiding my presence. Today I'm the prince of preparation!

From early spring it's been practice, practice, practice. Like an NCAA player perfecting his foul shot, I have fired my bow, calculated windage, reloaded, and released the string until it's second nature. Right here, right now, on the scale of one to ten, I'm a heavy ten. No room for mistakes, miscalculation, or muddin' up this moment.

The morning minutes pass, and I wait. To occupy my time, I count the species of trees around me. It's simply amazing how many kinds of trees live together in harmony—red oak, persimmon, white oak, ash, maple, cedar…the list could go on and on. How do so many different types live together out here without hindering each other? They just seem to stand silently, wave occasionally, and let everybody be what God made them to be. Maybe we humans could learn a lesson from them. But back to the opening-day hunt.

It's been an okay morning so far. I was hoping for more action by now, more than watching little lives scurry through the undergrowth, hearing sounds I haven't heard since my last attendance to this concert. But no heavy steps, the kind I want to hear. Then, as I mildly complain, something different makes a sound—a surprising yet recognizable note in this song of the woods. Yes, that's it…one, two, three, four steps in sync—heavy—behind me and getting closer.

My heart starts to beat like a bass drum in a high school marching band. If it doesn't stop thumping, I fear that every creature in the woodlands will hear it and run for cover. He's getting closer but moving to my right a bit. A careful glimpse—it's him. Oh, mercy—it's him!

I've seen him before. Actually, not for real, not in the flesh. I've only seen his leavings. The rubs, scrapes, marble-size droppings, and hoofprints have helped me paint a picture of this brute on the canvas of my daydreams. As he steps past my perch thirty yards out, I realize he's bigger than I thought. This is it. Take your time. The grunt call brought him in. Or maybe it was the doe-in-heat scent I put on my boot that led him to me. Whatever the genius, this is it!

Steady. Aim. Hold my breath. Peep-sight pin in place…release!

My heart stops as he disappears into the morning. I mark every tree and brush as he passes by each one. I take a photo in my mind of the last trunk I saw when he went out of sight, the one with a knot two feet off the ground. That's where he disappeared and where I will begin following the blood drops that will lead me into the record books. I don't think he went far.

But I've learned in the past that big deer have a heart that won't soon quit. Arriving at the knot tree within a minute of the shot (because I knew he couldn't see me dismount), I stop to consider my track-and-trail strategy. I'll check the color, the texture, the amount of red pool that tells the tale of where the razors met fur.

Suddenly, a crash a short distance away sounds like a felled tree. It's him, I'm sure. Sounded to me like he went down.

Working my way through the timber, checking the red trail and scanning the ground level, I arrive to find something much less welcome than expected. Instead of a body, I see another pool of redness. I recognize the dreaded sign. My shoulders droop; it's going to be a long day.

I'm no longer hunting for a boost to my reputation, nor for a place in the record books, nor for a 160-inch rack on the wall to prove greatness. Instead, it's become a matter of ethics and integrity. Now it's a case of enlisting some serious hunting character and testing my patience and endurance. Sit down…wait an hour, maybe two…the story of the hunt is not finished.

The next few hours will determine my state of mind and sense of worth, and I know that what happens will have a profound effect on what I'll feel when I lay my head on my pillow tonight. I can't give up. I can't quit. I'll crawl to find sign if necessary—and I do. The truth is clear, the sign is sure. He's wounded. The words sting my lips but finally I say them out loud.

"He's gut shot!"

Maybe he moved the split second I released. Maybe a branch or small sapling I didn't see deflected my arrow. Whatever the reason, the hunt is far from over and will definitely take some extra effort I didn't expect.

There are two kinds of hunters—those who *have* faced the dilemma of only wounding an animal and those who *will* face it. Perhaps you know how it feels because you've been there too. You realize that although you did your best—waited for the right moment, assured yourself it was a clear path for your bullet or broadhead to the deer's vitals—something went terribly wrong. The hit was amiss, and you had a wounded and crippled quarry to search for. All that matters now is finding your game ethically and, if necessary, quickly completing the kill and doing it with integrity to finish the hunt.

But every hunter knows the first step in finding a wounded beast is giving it time to weaken to the point of dying. That's what I must do now. I lean against an oak, remove the thermos lid, pour a cup, sip some steamy brew, and bide my time.

As I often do when I'm sitting and waiting, I meander down the many thought trails that sitting still can yield. One of those paths leads me to imagine what the deer is feeling right now. And it hurts to think about it. Knowing that his kind of hurt is worse, the hurt in my heart gets stronger. It seems that the sadness I'm feeling on this Saturday morning is erasing all the joy I felt yesterday.

Then, as I imagine his path of pain, I see a picture in it that I've never seen before. I realize this hunt has found me because I see myself in it. Like the sickened buck that struggles somewhere not too far away, there was a time in my life when childhood abandonment and abuse left me emotionally gut shot, wounded like the buck I needed to find. And I'm not the only one who was so wounded.

There are hunters in cities, woodlands, suburbs, and countrysides who have also been gut shot, so to speak. They've been sliced by the cruel and sharp arrows of life and may have been forgotten, hopeless, without anyone searching for them. Some may have even been abandoned to emotionally suffer and die. Many are the hunters who hurt and have had no one to come along and show them compassion or make any attempt to help or heal.

If you are one of those wounded ones, let me assure you that there is help through the One who knows exactly where you are, who knows how you feel, and who is fully able to heal your pain. He is the One who is reaching out to you and can find you—not to finish you off like a wounded deer, but to heal your wound no matter what caused it.

Maybe the arrow of abuse has left you feeling helpless and alone. Perhaps your parents or a spouse has abandoned you. Maybe you're a single parent who has been left with the sole responsibility of raising your children, or perhaps some other weapon of heartache has left you gut shot. If so, I have great news.

God, our Great Physician, says to all who are hurting, "My Son, Jesus, was wounded for your sins and bruised for your pain. The weight of your peace was upon Him, and through His stripes you are healed" (Isaiah 53:5, my paraphrase).

All this He did that you and I might live. He was wounded that we could be healed. He bore our sin on a cross so that we would never have to die, but could live forever with Him.

Rest assured wherever you are and however terribly you are wounded that He has the power to save, heal, and restore you. He can mend all the parts of your life that the arrows of sorrow have ripped through.

Let Him heal you. In this moment, let Him do it. Whisper to Him, "O Lord, come to me today. Find me, save me, heal me. In Jesus's name, I ask it."

If you've done this, now you may rejoice, for you have been found. You're alive because of Him!

Returning to the hunt for the wounded buck, an hour has passed, and all the coffee is gone. My ponderings about the hunted and wounded humans and my prayers for them are paused, and I begin the search for the wounded animal. After about an hour of methodically scanning the earth for a sign or a significant trail, at last I find the mighty four-footed warrior. Relief, sadness, joy, victory, defeat— all these emotions are mixed in the blender of my spirit in equal measure.

The day has not been as perfect as I'd planned, but it ended respectfully. And to have failed in retrieving this king of the woodlands would have been nothing short of an absolutely failed mission of mercy.

In the evening following dinner, and after my bride graciously and patiently listens as I tell and retell the story of the hunt, I lay my head down on my pillow in the dark. In the quiet I can't stop my mind from wandering back to the gut-shot buck and how it must have hurt before it died. Then once again I think of the human wounded ones whose souls are so hurt. Compassion for them washes over me, and I feel a new determination to hunt for, find, and rescue as many wounded and weary souls as I can. Until I do, I pray.

Father, have mercy on those who have been hurt, who've been wounded and maybe left to struggle alone. Would You, in this moment, let them feel Your presence and hear Your voice? Lord, speak in a language they understand, and help them hear You whisper healing words. Help each one who feels lost and forgotten to call out to You today, and assure them that You will find them and restore them to new life through the mighty work of Christ in their hearts. Thank You, Father. In Christ's name I pray. Amen.

Oh, what an unforgettable opening day it's been!

THE HURTING PATH

If I could have had but one granted wish
It would have been not to hurt like this
I would have chosen the clear, smooth path
And escaped the climb of this mountain's wrath
Not to have felt this awful pain
But to avoid the storm, for the gentle rain
Nor feel the sting of being used
For other's pleasure, to have been abused
To drink the dregs of this bitter cup
Not just a portion, but fully turned up

And then a memory at my mind's door
Of one who walked in pain before
Who, on His road, had known no bed
To lie upon or rest His head
The One, I'm told, whose love found me
Thru many years, my hurt would see
Who knelt alone in a garden place
As sweat like blood dripped down His face
Who cried, "If I could have but one granted wish
It would have been not to hurt like this
I would have chosen the clear, smooth path
And escaped the climb of this mountain's wrath"
So Lord, if my pain You clearly see
Send somebody soon to rescue me
From hidden hurt and sheltered strife
To find a purpose for living life
From the hurting path to finally be
A wounded hunter, healed, set free[1]

6

Take a Stand

STEVE

If you say the words "It's time to take a stand" to a serious hunter during an open season, he or she may break into a big smile and suddenly turn on their heels, go to their gear room, put on some camo and boots, toss a bow or gun in their vehicle, and head to the woods. I expect that would be my response. You just have to be careful not to say it when season is not in. You could get me in trouble with the game wardens in our county.

There's a good explanation for why many of my friends and I instantly connect "take a stand" with hunting. It's because of how we're wired. We think, breathe, smell, eat, talk, and walk the fair chase. If we're not out there doing it, we're planning on doing it, strategizing how we're going to do it, figuring out how we can afford to do it, and trying to convince somebody that for the sake of our sanity we can't afford not to do it. (God help the spouses!)

Hunters don't apologize for the king-size "want to" we constantly feel when it comes to hunting. What others say doesn't matter to us. Our battle cry is, "A-hunting we will go!" Of course, the smart ones among us are aware that such a strong commitment to our obsession requires us to be careful not to alienate our loved ones by spending way too much time and money to do it. We care what our family thinks and feels about our passion, but how others outside our circle of love view us is simply a moot point.

I've had a few confrontations with anti-hunting folks in the past. For example, I received a letter from a hater of hunters after he, or maybe she, saw the cover of one of my books on a shelf in an airport gift shop. When the writer mentioned the title, *A Look at Life from a Deer Stand*, I knew the cover photo they had seen. Standing in the picture is an impressive, New York State whitetail buck photographed by the legendary Charles Alsheimer. It's an eye-catching picture for sure.

I can only assume that it wasn't the incredibly beautiful photo of the deer that drew the ire of the letter writer. It was likely the words "Deer Stand" that were prominent on the cover. Also, I suspect the subtitle generated a reaction: *Hunting for the Meaning of Life*. I guess they must have exploded with anger when they saw the combination of the photo and the suggestion in the title and subtitle that something good for the soul could come from hunting and killing an animal. The proof of their fury was in the word bullets loaded in the letter. It said something like this:

> I won't call you sir because you don't deserve to be respected. How could you possibly call yourself a godly man when you maim and kill such lovely creatures? You

should be ashamed of murdering them, and in fact, I hope you fall out of one of your stands. Maybe it would stop you from doing such a despicable thing as hunting.

I was not about to respond to the letter, which, by the way, was anonymous. Nor was there a need to do so. I've found that to argue with an "anti" is futile. (If I did write back, I'd simply ask, "Do you own a pair of leather shoes?" 'Nuff said.)

Where do hunters like me, and likely you since you're reading these stories, find the courage to ignore and dismiss the negativity about the thing we love to do? Does it come from a hatred for those who spew anti-hunting venom? I don't think so because most of us view them as pitiful people with misguided affections who are actually missing something exciting they could do with their time.

Is our courage found in our firepower, in knowing we can defend ourselves against them if they decided to express their anger with violence? No. The "antis" would be surprised to know that most hunters are gentle at heart and that the very last thing we'd want to do is unload on our fellow man.

Some hunters quip that we have a biblical mandate to hunt, referring to Acts 10:13, where the apostle Peter was told to "rise…kill and eat." We enjoy the humorous take on the verse, but that's not what ultimately causes us to boldly ignore the "anti" rhetoric that's thrown at us and then go hunting anyway. So what is our source of courage? I'll speak for myself.

The main reason I'm not deterred from going hunting by people like the mean-spirited letter writer is simple. My Maker has used hunting to make me a better man. I have an immense sense of gratitude to God for being kind to teach me some of life's most important lessons through His awesome creation and the creatures in it. I've learned about the necessity of living on the alert by a wise old

West Virginia buck. I've developed endurance and patience while climbing a steep Montana mountain in search of black bear. The opportunities to grow stronger in character have been many. I've filled books with the insights my awesome God has shown me, and if only for that reason, I have nothing but good to say about hunting.

But I have other reasons not to be ashamed of hunting. The great food source it represents, the friendships that come from it, and the commerce that hunting generates are just a few. I keep all these benefits on the tip of my tongue, ready to use them as a defense of hunting if needed. But there's one more reason I'm so glad my blood runs blaze orange. My willingness to defend hunting has been a good training ground for courageously taking a stand for an even greater cause—the name of Christ.

I believe that Jesus is the Son of the Living God and the One who cleansed my sinful heart with His shed blood. But I live in a world filled with people who hate Him, so I am aware that being His follower puts me at odds with the anti-Christians. Regardless of the consequences, I must be faithful to Him. He is supremely worthy of my complete loyalty, and He has won my heart with His vast and unconditional love. For that reason, I will not be silenced when it comes to Christ.

If you were to point to the woods on a bright, cool, sunny afternoon and say to the hunter in me, "It's time to take a stand," you will definitely see me get excited. But I want to be even more excited and ready if you point to the dark clouds of hate for Christ that have gathered over our culture and say to me, "It's time to take a stand." When I do, I'll be in good company, considering the two great men of faith whose story in the third and fourth chapters of the book of Acts is told in the following lyric.

WE'RE GONNA TALK ABOUT JESUS

Peter and John were on their way up to the temple
When they prayed in Jesus's name and God healed a cripple
The rulers and lawyers didn't like what they did, so they jailed
   them
And said, "Don't use that name around here, it's not welcome"

But they said, "We can't stop talking 'bout Jesus
There's just too much to tell
He's the one who died to save us
And He made that crippled man well
You can put us on trial for saying the name
Of the One who died to redeem us
Do what you will, but we won't be still
We're gonna talk about Jesus

After two thousand years it appears not much is different
The name of Christ still offends, and many don't want to hear it
Our courts and our makers of law want us all to be quiet
But just like Peter and John, we won't be silent[2]

7

The New Guy

DON

I believe that anytime I meet someone new, there's a purpose for it. Sometimes they need what I can offer. Sometimes, however, I need what they can offer. Thank God I met a fellow hunter named Jim.

In my earlier days of chasing whitetails, my attitude could have been best described as bloodthirsty. For me, the joy of a deer hunt was a hard hit on the hair just above and behind the front shoulder, followed by some crashing and thrashing in the bed of leaves where the animal fell. Several friends and I shared that mindset, and each year we'd meet up at the same camp. We would exchange stories of previous exploits and engage in a discussion about who would win the season's "tag and brag" contest. It was always the same crowd and the same competitive atmosphere. I loved it.

That's how it started almost thirty years ago. If there was no meat in the locker at the end of the day, the hunt had been fruitless, a failure. Camping, cooking, conversation, and camouflage were not the main mission—killing was. Venison equaled victory.

Then one year, one of the hunters invited a new guy named Jim to join us. He had the right camo, a hi-tech bow with all the latest gadgets, and most important, lots of tasty pastries to share.

One thing I noticed that Jim didn't do was add to the prehunt trash talk about why and how he'd be the first to poke a hole in a big buck. Instead, he just listened to the rest of us do it. He seemed pleasant and friendly enough, but when someone new joins up and they seem a little reserved, a fellow just has to "figger 'em out."

Silently the questions crossed my mind. *Is Jim the kind of hunter who would follow me secretly to find my best place? Would he go back when no one would know and hunt my best spot?* I just wasn't sure. All I knew was that he seemed a bit strange to me, especially following cleanup after our first dinner when he wandered off into the dark by himself without letting us know where he went or why. He wasn't gone a long time, just enough to feed my suspicions.

The area we had permission to hunt was about 150 acres, which meant the distance between our stands was not so great that we wouldn't be heard if we yelled for help after a deer was down. Even though I wasn't quite sure yet about our newcomer, I'll admit that it was a good thing to have Jim there as another pair of ears, another strong back, and an extra pair of hands to help with trackin', guttin', and draggin'.

On the second morning of our hunt, I climbed into my elevated overlook, and it wasn't long until a mature doe came browsing through the woods. I could already taste the teriyaki jerky strips and plump tenderloins! I drew my string back when she was at twenty yards and waited for the perfect broadside shot. The result was cold steel in the hot boiler room. No doubt about it, she was done. After a short wait, knowing I had closed the deal, I slowly descended from my tree throne and began the short walk to complete the mission and retrieve the dead deer.

Finding her about 100 yards away, I proudly hollered for a little guttin' help. It was the new guy who showed up. When I saw him coming toward me I thought, *I knew it! He followed me to map out my best stand tree.* But when he spoke, it was shock time.

"She walked right by me at ten yards," Jim said.

"Did you miss her?" I hoped he could detect the sarcasm in my question.

"Nope," he said, "I just let her walk."

"Why?"

"Well...she was just so beautiful."

There seemed to be no apologetic tone in his answer, just confidence. Surprised by it, I stuttered and stumbled a bit to verbally react.

"Beautiful?" I asked, hoping Jim would detect my doubt. "Man, she's a deer! We're deer hunters. These aren't watching woods; these are killing woods."

"I know," Jim said. "But sometimes I just like to enjoy the beauty. Not that I wouldn't shoot a deer...just not this one. Congrats to you though."

I didn't say much more as Jim helped me finish the field-dressing job, tag her, and drag her to my truck. After check-in and locker delivery, I hurried to get back to camp to relish the kudos from the crowd. After all, I had first-blood bragging rights.

Jim had already returned to camp, so I assumed he had told the others what had happened, and my account would be a replay.

Oddly though, Jim hadn't told anyone. He pulled me aside and quietly said, "No one knows you got one…I didn't want to steal your thunder. I just told them I saw you in the field and you would be along sooner or later."

I couldn't figure him out at all.

That night I decided to secretly follow Jim after we had dinner to wherever it was he wandered off to when he went outside. He didn't go that far really, just a few steps out of eyesight and earshot. I stopped abruptly when I heard him talking. I thought he had seen me and was speaking to me, but I was wrong. He was actually on his knees on the damp ground. I felt awkward lingering, but I listened long enough to hear him say something I'll never forget. He offered thanks to God for "giving Mr. Don a deer."

I never did know if he was aware I had eavesdropped on him that night, but after hearing his prayer I knew I really liked the new guy. I snuck away with a whole new outlook on his gentle, easygoing personality, and I set my sights on getting to know him better.

Jim and I ended up talking a lot after that. I learned about his life, his marriage, his three children, and how God had blessed his family through the years. He also talked about his gratitude for Christ, about Calvary, and about how his Savior died so that people like him and me could live in peace. Without flinching he shared how God chose to love me before I ever knew I needed His love. I listened willingly and later realized the wisdom of God's plan to deliver such a life-changing message to a hunter through a hunter. Because of that message, my life and my home were changed.

Our friendship grew beyond the hunting camp, and I looked forward to seeing "the new guy" the following October. But not long before opening day of the new season, in the middle of the night, Jim felt some chest pain. His family later called me to tell me he was ill, and I drove as fast as I could to be with them. I sat and talked with him for a while that night when he was having some discomfort. I didn't know it would be our last conversation.

Hunting season arrived the following year, and the group met up again—without Jim. It was a little quieter in the camp. On the first morning I was surprised to see a very mature eight-pointer with a wide spread standing broadside about twenty yards away. He was a buck we hunters often refer to as a taker, but not that day. Why? Because I couldn't help but imagine that Jim was watching. I thought, *Maybe next time I'll take the shot—just not this time.* Things were different. I was different.

The heavy buck walked slowly away, and the last thing I saw as he disappeared over the hill was the tips of his tall rack. I looked upward and whispered, "Hey, new guy in heaven, this time I chose to see the beauty."

MASTER OF THE MORNING

Now there he stands with shining rack, the master of his race,
And I with sharpened steel and bow held sure in perfect place.
The hidden stand among the limbs, I knew he could not see.
Is this the hour I've waited for, his life be given to me?
Just one more step, I spoke in silence, and season will be ended.
The wisdom of his many years, his life has not defended.
Now as he stands, that one step taken, his blood about to spill,
My mind slips back two thousand years to a tree on another hill.
His head hung low, His eyes look tired, to give those men a thrill,
The nails, the spear, like arrows cast, about to close the deal.
And then I saw that Master's eyes turn and look at me,

"You're the master of the morning, what will your choice now be?
What did God do when in His eyes your sin left you alone?"
Then deep inside where no one sees, the thrill of death was gone.
Another time, another day, he and I in another place.
The blood today, it's in my soul, and a chorus, "Amazing Grace."[3]

8

Where Are My Children?

STEVE

Sometimes a scene in the wild touches a place inside me that goes deeper than normal. When it happens there's usually something about it that's very personal.

In early bow season in our part of the world, the fawns are still very attached to their moms. They were born in late May or early June, so when the first day of the season arrives in late September or the first week of October, the young ones are only about four months old. In most cases their spots are still visible, and they haven't been fully weaned.

Even a rough, old, die-hard bow hunter who climbs into a tree stand or slips into a ground blind for the purpose of filling a deer tag can be softened by the sight of a caring doe and her tender fawns. At least it was true for me one unforgettable morning.

It was an unusually chilly dawn in the second week of September, and when the sun lit up the woods enough to see well, I was surprised to notice my breath forming a mist. It was way too early in the fall for that to happen. I began to toy with the vapor by trying to make rings with it and didn't notice the doe and a pair of spotted "young'uns" coming down the hill to my right. I didn't know they were approaching until I heard the subdued sound of their footsteps about twenty-five yards away.

Ten seconds after I saw the trio, they stopped right under me. The doe suddenly got nervous. Her tail twitched and her ears rotated like radar as she listened intently for the sound of whatever it was she had detected with her very keen nose. She raised her head a little to smell the dead-still air. What a sight…and she hadn't yet busted me.

I had a drone's-eye view of a mother who was now on full alert. She turned her head to see her fawns, and they were watching her intently. They didn't blink as they studied their mother's behavior. The siblings were instantly in the survival classroom for inexperienced whitetails.

Maybe it was a downdraft I couldn't feel or perhaps some sort of sixth sense the doe possessed that made her begin anxiously stomping the ground with her front right hoof. Whatever it was that caused it, I assumed she realized I was very close. The next thing that happened was impressive. She snorted and at the same time used her powerful legs to go airborne. She came down at least ten feet away from where she had been standing. Amazing.

Startled by the sudden commotion, her two fawns darted several yards back in the direction they had come and stopped to see what their mama was going to do. Because she didn't run after she landed, it was apparent she wasn't sure what the odor was that had invaded her olfactory system. Maybe she was confused by the raw-earth-scent cover wafer I had pinned to my hat, or maybe it was my breath, which smelled like the apple slice I was sucking on. I couldn't say. But I was certain she wouldn't hang around much longer.

There seemed to be an expression of worry on her face as she looked for her little ones. It was as if she were thinking, *Where are my children?* When she saw them, she seemed to calm for a few seconds and then continued cautiously searching the area for something out of the ordinary.

The doe was so unnerved, she snorted again at a decibel level that rivaled a train whistle. Her loud protest was immediately followed by another series of snorts and a quick, determined run back up the hillside to my right. Trailing behind her were her two students. I watched her go about sixty yards and then stop and look back as if to say, "You two are way too slow. Move it." Twenty seconds later I was still watching them when she began a kind of stuttered, cautious walk that led her babies out of sight to a safer place.

I don't suppose deer think like humans, but I am convinced they have emotional reactions. The mother doe I watched that morning definitely appeared to feel threatened, especially because her fawns were close by.

As I sat in my stand, admiring the protective attitude the doe displayed, I thought, *Some moms and dads in my species sure could benefit from the kind of alert parental care I just witnessed.* I'm proud and grateful to say that when our two "fawns" were in our home, my dear wife was as attentive to them as the doe was to her two offspring. I was especially made aware of it one Sunday after morning worship at church.

Annie escorted our son and daughter to the basement of the building, where children's church was held, and then joined me in the sanctuary, where I was saving her a place in a pew. When the service started we both glanced at each other with a look that said, *Isn't it nice not to be distracted by the kids?* Honestly, we enjoyed the break.

Though we were free birds for the moment, I noticed Annie got very quiet during the singing and then didn't respond much throughout the rest of the service. On the way home she told me what had happened that made her so pensive. I'll never forget what she said.

"During the singing I had…for lack of a better word, a vision of sorts. It's like I was transported to a place I imagined was Jerusalem. It seemed so real, I could almost taste the dust in the air. The two of us were sitting on the ground under a tree, listening to a robed man teach. I felt in my heart that it was Jesus mainly because He had a couple of children on his lap and several other little ones sitting around him."

Annie had my full attention at this point. I couldn't wait to hear the rest of what had been on her mind.

"All at once the man stopped teaching, looked straight at me, and asked, 'Where are your children?' I answered, 'They're downstairs in children's church.' Then he said something that will change my Sundays from now on."

I was a little nervous to know what she heard, but I asked, "And what did He say?"

Annie looked at our two very young kids sitting in the backseat of our car and answered, "He asked me, 'Why are your children not sitting at My feet?' At that moment I was transported back to the pew we were sitting in. It was so real."

Chills ran up and down my spine when I heard what Annie shared with me. I knew in my heart of hearts that she had received some instruction regarding our son and daughter that we shouldn't ignore. From that Sunday on, our kids were to be with us in what we eventually started calling "big church." They learned how to sit and listen at the feet of the pastor, who spoke on behalf of the One teaching under the tree in the scene that Annie envisioned.

The next Sunday, the four of us gathered in a pew for the morning service. It felt good to be obedient to what we considered to be a divine directive, but it wasn't easy. The kids were not conditioned to sit still, but we managed to make it happen—partly at the expense of a few saints who sat near us and endured the extra movement and noise, and partly at the expense of our patience.

Over time, Annie and I learned how to sing and listen to the preacher with kids on our laps (eating their Cheerios), and they learned how to sit still. By the time they were teenagers, they were so used to being with us in big church, they didn't want to go to the youth service during that hour. We were proud of them for wanting to hear what the pastor had to say and grateful for their compliant attitude. We're convinced they're better people for it today.

Like an alert doe responding to warning signs and helping her fawns escape danger, Annie took her Sunday morning "vision" as a warning. Unwilling to risk what might happen if she didn't make sure her children were "sitting at the feet of Jesus," she became an odd doe in the church herd. Other mothers questioned our decision to pull our kids out of children's church, and some even ridiculed us for it. Annie was careful to tell those who were puzzled, worried, or offended by our choice that she had nothing against the downstairs children's activities, but we would do what seemed good for our family.

Perhaps the imagery of the mother doe that seemed so worried about where her fawns were when she sensed trouble in her woods reminds you of the kind of parent you want to be in the face of looming danger. Or maybe the question the gentle Savior asked Annie in her envisioned encounter with Him is one you know you need to answer. If so, don't hesitate to ask yourself, *Where are my children?* It's the wise thing to do.

9

Downtime

DON

With only a few minutes remaining before the "great ball of fire" rose in the east and lit up the woods around my tree stand, I relished the feeling of my nerves relaxing. Oh, how I needed some time away from the woes of the marketplace, a few hours of not having a worry in the world. But I found out that day that downtime has its hazards.

Before shooting light arrived, I was already feeling so comfortable that my eyes began to droop. I was more in need of a break than I thought. Before I allowed myself the luxury of deer-stand slumber, I remembered a policy that I had self-imposed years earlier. *No sleeping in an elevated stand.* I knew I had to follow my own advice—or else.

Knowing about the injuries that can be caused by falling asleep while suspended above the earth in a deer stand, I considered lowering my weapon quietly to the ground, descending from my lofty paradise, taking a seat next to the tree with my back leaning against the trunk, and simply taking a long nap. It was the safer thing to do, but I didn't do it for one good reason that only a diehard hunter will understand. As sure as the world is round, while I slumbered, a trophy buck could walk within five feet of me, and I'd wake up just in time to hear the echo of his snorting laughter as he ran off.

As much as I could have used the rest, I decided to stay in the tree stand and stay awake. I needed downtime, but I didn't need falling-down time. To help me keep my eyes open, I took note of an entire host of woodland guests as they begin to stir. I heard things tweeting, singing, crawling in the leaves below me, and swinging on the limbs above me. It was a great postdawn show, and as I enjoyed it, across the narrow field I suddenly caught the sight of something that nearly took my breath away.

Just inside the edge of the woods across from me stood a huge deer. With its size, weight, and rack height, it could have been featured on one of those "monster buck" TV hunting shows. I had to remind myself to whisper instead of yell as I counted the tines.

"One, two, three…" I kept counting until all the points were numbered. Finally, through my barely controlled excitement I spoke to myself. "Man…it's a wide twelve pointer!"

The buck just stood there. From my point of view, it seemed that before stepping into the open field, he had to assure himself that nothing would hinder his travel from his side of the field to where I sat waiting. I quietly begged him to move—as if he could hear me.

He stood like a statue while my nerves wobbled like Jell-O. His pose seemed calm and collected on the outside, but I had studied deer enough to know that his emotions were likely wired tighter than piano strings. He was ready to respond to the slightest abnormality in his surroundings. No doubt he had stood on that same spot many times before in both daylight and dark, calculating his next step. He was not allowing himself to have any downtime. He was on full alert.

I wondered if the buck's keen awareness of endless possibilities of danger was a trait that was passed down to him genetically. Or did his mother teach him this when he was a spotted youngster? Did his dad teach him the wily ways of forest living and the inherent hazards in the worn trail that crossed the meadow?

By whatever means the buck had learned to be alert, I could see he was applying the lessons as he remained as still as a statue. But then he took a few steps. When he did, my heart raced like an Indy car engine. He dropped his nose to the dew-covered clover as if he would have some breakfast. It appeared that he felt safe, that he was ready for some downtime in the cafeteria. I was wrong. His head was down only a couple of seconds before he raised it immediately to look around and make sure nothing within sight had moved. One thing was for certain—he was far from relaxed.

Years ago an old experienced hunter with whom I spent many days in the woods told me, "Don't ever forget…the dumb deer are already dead." That's why the buck I was watching was alive and well. He was no dummy. But thanks to the guidance of older hunters like my aging friend, I was no dummy either. I had been taught well by my sage mentor, and as the motionless buck tampered with my nerves I thought of something else he taught me.

"A mature buck's greatest weakness is when his greatest strength is left unprotected." We see one of the best examples of this bit of wisdom during rut season. Most deer hunters know that a normally woods-wise male deer can act insane when the females become "interested." He totally forsakes his normally cautious nature for the sake of hooking up with the girls in the local herd. Basically, he fails to maintain or protect his cautious attitude and exchanges it for a chance at "love."

Does that dangerous lapse in judgment sound familiar to you? Sure it does, especially if you're a man who is alive and breathing. We "human bucks" have the potential to be just as crazy when it comes to dealing with our attraction to women. In most cases, we get in trouble when we believe we're strong enough to control our eyes, thoughts, and actions but fail to consciously enlist those strengths when temptation comes. When might that happen? Here's an example.

Jack is traveling for the weekend by himself. He checks into a motel room and settles in for the night. He grabs the remote and starts flipping through the channels. Suddenly, there's "that" channel. The skin that appears on the screen is not covered, and there's lots of it. In that moment he says to himself, *I'm strong enough to take in a few seconds of this stuff.* Bam…he just shot his morals with the "I can handle this" gun. It happened because for a moment he left his strength unprotected and unused. Who knows what that mistake might lead to? Get the picture?

As I continued the standoff with the big guy, I was relieved to see him start to move. His steps were careful and deliberate. I could tell he really was a smart one. He seemed a little reluctant to cross the meadow, as if he knew he'd be fully exposed. Still, he headed in my direction on the well-traveled path he had safely traveled so many times before. I assumed the fallen acorns under the oak trees behind me were on his mind.

At last he made it across and stopped at the edge of the woods on my side, but he was still out of arrow range. Just before he moved again he looked intently into the shaded woods. I assumed he was just making sure that nothing was out of place, that the landscape hadn't changed, and that other critters were busy with their normal activities.

When he sensed that he had an all-clear status, he stepped into the leaves of his hallowed refuge, and I began my master plan. Having had the time to stand up and get ready for a shot, I watched him cautiously approach. I was already in position to close the deal.

There he was, and…oh wow! I realized I had miscounted. *He's not a twelve, he's a fourteen!* I hadn't seen the three-inch, scorable stickers on each side. My breath created a nearly transparent fog that rolled from the side of my mouth. If I hadn't seen the floating mist I would have questioned whether I was breathing.

It was time for full draw. I had to make sure he was looking away. No room for a mistake now. As I prepared to find him in my peep sight, I wondered if he was the one I had seen the previous season and had waited a year to see again.

Then another sound got my attention. I slowly turned to my left only to see a huge doe standing there looking nervous. My thoughts swirled. *So that's why he came across the field. Where did she come from? Did she see me move? Has she winded me? Will she tell him I'm here?*

She stomped the ground with her front hoof—she knew I was there. Before I could turn my eyes back to the buck that awaited my arrow, he bolted away, and that was that. I lowered my bow and processed the few previous moments.

A dream buck was there one instant and gone the next. I had a spot already picked out over my fireplace for the fourteen-point mount. I can't tell you how devastated I felt.

Though I didn't get to drag the monster home, I did put a tag on a sizable trophy of another kind. The mature buck had relaxed his cautious nature when he saw the doe, and it almost cost him his life. The same thing can happen to me when it comes to my spiritual life.

How true it is that downtime, especially when it comes to our relationships with women, definitely has its dangers. That's what Jack was dealing with in his hotel room. When a man lets his guard down, the devil lets the arrows fly.

I don't know about you, but I don't want to be a victim of spiritual downtime. God knows my physical body needs the rest, but never my spirit. Never. Here's what I hope and pray for myself and for you too.

God, help us to be sober, vigilant, watchful, and careful. Help us live in such a way that we will have many tomorrows filled with memories of good decisions. Walk before us as our guide, behind us as our rear guard, beside us as our dearest friend, above us to watch over our ways, and within us to teach our hearts to walk in Your truths so that our days will be filled with peace. In the name of Christ, may it be so.

10

Expect the Unexpected

STEVE

Hunting has taught me at least one good way to be prepared for whatever life throws at me. I've learned to expect the unexpected. This lesson is well illustrated in a story about a bear hunter.

I was the invited guest speaker at a wild-game dinner event in a northeastern state, and I looked forward to enjoying the meal with the attendees. After the prayer of thanks, I filled my plate with venison, squirrel, and even a taste of groundhog. I added some French fries to the pile to make sure I got my daily veggie requirement. When I reached the end of the self-service line, I grabbed a tall cup of sweet iced tea and turned around to scan the room for a table with an empty chair.

I like to learn something about the communities I visit as well as the local hunting, so I sit with folks who are from the area. I saw a table for six with only five guys around it, so I headed their way and sat down with them. As they chowed, they were doing something I thoroughly enjoy. They were swapping stories. One of them was unforgettable. My fellow table-dude prefaced his tale with a disclaimer.

"I didn't live this hunt, and I'm glad I didn't. I heard about it from a friend at work. He had a buddy who had been bow hunting for several years. He had taken a lot of deer and even an elk out west, but he'd never gone after black bear."

At that point I had not had a chance to hunt bear with gun or bow and had wondered what it would be like. So I was curious about what I was about to hear. The story continued.

"This guy went on a hunt that involved setting up his portable climber in a tree over a bait barrel. Nothing happened the first day. On day two he saw a couple of smaller males he didn't want to take. Finally, on the third day of a four-day hunt, he saw the black bear he definitely wanted, but he had no idea how dangerously close he'd end up getting to it."

Five of us at the table chewed as quietly as possible so we wouldn't miss a word.

"About nine in the morning, a mature boar that looked heavy and healthy came wandering out of the brush to the bait barrel under him. For the first five minutes, it fed while facing the tree and didn't offer the broadside shot.

"Finally the boar circled the barrel and ended up on the left side of it in just the right position for a lethal shot at its lungs. The hunter raised his bow and found the bear's vitals in his peep sight. The arrow covered the twenty yards in a flash and then disappeared in the coal-black fur."

It's an interesting thing that hunters can tell such gruesome details while at a dinner table and never miss a bite. Along with the others I continued eating and couldn't wait to hear what happened next.

"I was told that the bear jumped when it felt the impact of the arrow, and instead of running off into the woods like the guy thought it would, it acted completely confused and ran straight to the tree the hunter was in. Much to his surprise, the bear dug its claws into the bark and began climbing. The guy was stunned and didn't know what to do except sit still and hope for the best."

I stopped eating. I didn't notice whether anyone else did too.

"The bear seemed to have a lot of strength to climb in spite of having a broadhead pass through it. Thankfully, it was on the opposite side of the trunk from the hunter. He couldn't believe it when the bear shimmied up the tree past him. It even used the rear of the stand platform as a foothold as it went up. It climbed out on a wide limb about eight feet above the hunter. He could hear it breathing heavily and detected a bit of gurgle in his throat as it breathed. It sounded like a death rattle."

By then, the only thing I was consuming at the table were a few sips of water. My thoughts ran wild as I imagined sitting in a climber with a heavy, dying bear directly above my head. What next?

"Blood started dripping on the guy's cap and then falling on his shoulders and the bib of his camo coveralls. He knew that life was draining from the bear, and suddenly it hit him that when the bear died, it was going to come tumbling off the limb and right onto his lap. He realized he had to make a move and do it fast."

I tried to quickly guess what the hunter would do in that situation, but before I could figure something out, the man across the table finished the story.

"The guy was in one of those two-piece stands, and as he stood to make a life-saving maneuver, he could only hope the bear was sick enough not to care about the movement below. He hurriedly turned around, found his feet straps, slid his boots into them, sat down on the rail facing the tree, and lifted the platform to unlock it from the trunk. Instead of descending to the ground, he quickly started working his climber around the tree a few inches at a time. His thinking was that if he got on the other side, he'd be out of the way when the bear's dead body tumbled off the limb. Just as he got around to the opposite side of the tree, he heard the bear let out a dying grunt, and that's when he saw a large mass of black fur flash downward, right where he had been sitting only moments earlier. His timing was perfect."

I shook my head and offered a stunned, "Whoa!" I was not alone. None of us could think of another word to say as we processed such a frightening near disaster. We were relieved to hear that the hunter, though drenched in blood, managed to escape injury. We also logged away a survival tip we could use the next time we found ourselves in a climber with a bleeding, dying bear precariously perched on a limb above us.

The story reminds us that hunting is a classroom where we can learn to expect the unexpected. When the bear hunter woke up that morning, he never could have planned for the challenge he would face and the fast thinking he would have to do in order to return home alive. I have a feeling that before he went to sleep that night, he said a prayer of thanks to God for delivering him from possibly being killed by the bear he killed.

The undeniable truth that it's wise to expect the unexpected reminds me of one of my all-time favorite lines in a song. It was written by friend and fellow hunter Lindsey Williams in a song we cowrote and titled "You Just Never Know (What a Day Will Bring)."

Sometimes life will lift up your soul
Sometimes life will lay you low
Not much is certain, but one thing is clear
You'll never live in the moment till it gets here[4]

The truth in Lindsey's line is absolute because it has biblical roots. Proverbs 27:1 (NIV) says, "Do not boast about tomorrow, for you do not know what a day may bring."

May God help us as we live and learn to deal with the unexpected events that life can toss our way. Whether it's danger or delight or anything in between that surprises us, may He give us clear minds to know how to react and especially whom to thank for the outcome when the day is done.

11

The Lost Hunter

DON

Being able to go hunting on my own little bit of geographical glory is a great blessing, but I also love finding new territory to explore. I can almost feel the spirit of Lewis and Clark as I trek into unfamiliar ground to find a secluded place to put a stand for the first time. The following is my remembrance of such a place.

If you were ever privileged to go to Rodney Holler and managed to find the old home there, you could stand on the front porch, look in all directions, and be swallowed by wilderness.

What made that property so inviting was that the Rodney family had moved out of the hollow and into town several years before I showed up, abandoning the vast acreage. Mr. Rodney had gotten a job in the town sawmill, so he and his family decided to move to where they had modern conveniences, such as city water and a nearby grocery store. They especially liked their mail being delivered right to their front door almost every day.

Most of the Rodney clan had lived in the hollow for generations. They tended to keep to themselves, didn't bother other folks, and expected the same in return. Some would have said they were hermits or perhaps just a backwoods band of country folk who didn't know what they were missing. The strange thing was that when I listened to some of my neighbors talk about the stresses of life, what the world was coming to, and the good old days, I would often hear one of them say, "We ought to go and live like the Rodneys. They don't have all these problems." Well, I guess the Rodneys felt the reverse of the matter, so town is where they ended up.

When folks in the area heard that the clan had abandoned the old home place, a few brave souls took the opportunity to venture into the once restricted area. Included in the curious few were hunters like me who had heard of a deer paradise that was once off-limits but was now open to those who were not afraid to venture through those dark mountains, raging streams, and natural booby traps. It was a dangerous place. A novice could get lost in those hills faster than the Andretti boys could turn a lap at the Indianapolis Speedway.

There were rumors that one of the young Rodneys had wandered into those deep hollows and had never come out. Some laid the blame for his disappearance on a hungry bear, others said a rattlesnake got him, and still others said it was simply a case of getting hopelessly turned around. As daunting as those speculations were, none of them dissuaded me from joining the handful of brave souls who chose to enter the Rodney region. Curiosity, the same magnet that killed many a cat, got the best of me.

The way I figured it was that I'd been in the woods all my life, and though I've been off course for a few hours a couple of times, I've never gotten myself hopelessly misplaced (at least I've never admitted it). Getting lost is for folks who don't know the business of negotiating new territory and ought not be outdoors anyway.

As I began to plan my trip to the newly accessible deer haven, one of the first things I decided was to go solo. I didn't want a companion, and I didn't want to risk anyone else learning about the place and spreading the word to other deer chasers. I wanted to do my part to make sure this private ground didn't become a public parking lot for tree stands.

When the alarm sounded early that unforgettable Tuesday morning, I awoke knowing two wonderful things. I had the entire rest of the week off, and I had completed my honey-do stuff on Monday. With so much time to enjoy and all my domestic responsibilities covered, I slipped out of bed, planted a light kiss on my wife's cheek, and headed out to discover the unfamiliar world of Rodney Holler.

The tent was packed, my backpack was stuffed with food galore, and my water container was nearly the size of a Volkswagen (and weighed as much). I had everything needed to survive the next five days. My gun and ammunition as well as my bow and fully loaded quiver were tucked under my arms. Yes, this was a two-weapon-option hunt. I was fully prepared. If my shafted arrows didn't do the trick, I'd be ready with a shaftless arrow from my .50 caliber "smoke pole."

I knew it would take most of the day to get deep into the hollow, set up camp, and be ready to bow hunt the first evening. I would have to scout a bit, pick an ambush location, and be ready and settled in by midafternoon. The next few days after that would be a breeze. All I needed was a perfectly placed stand and the patience to sit and wait.

Getting in the valley that afternoon and being a little surprised that I was misplaced a bit before finding the old Rodney home, I realized I was running a little late. Consequently, I had no time to set up camp, scout, and get settled in by hunting time. Being one who would rather hunt than eat or sleep, I made the decision that I could do a quick, scaled-down camp setup later with a flashlight. A protein bar would suffice for supper, and I'd do the rest in tomorrow's daylight after a morning of hunting—that is, if I hadn't already taken a Rodney Holler buck that first evening.

I dumped my stuff behind a huge stump out of sight of the old house and almost ran as I trekked deep into the woods. It didn't take a lot to figure out that the place was a deer heaven. Like a little boy in a toy store, I began just wandering around until I found fresh deer trails. There were plenty of them, and one in particular caught my eye. My heart pounded when I saw that it was beaten down like a well-used cow path. I attached my climbing stand to the base of a soft-bark tree overlooking the newly discovered whitetail highway and ascended to a height of nearly twenty feet. It was the perfect spot, and I was pumped full of anticipation.

As often happens when the setup seems perfect and the promise for sightings is at its highest, the setting sun brought a finale to my carefully executed plan. As if to tell me I was not the master of the fair chase, the big orange sphere gradually disappeared behind the western tree line. The day was ending.

I had seen some small bucks and a few nice does, but when a fellow is in a place like the Rodney ranch, settling for second-best is not an option. I was willing to wait for the boss buck. I'd have to come back tomorrow.

I knew I had a long walk back to where I left all my camping equipment and survival goods, so I dismounted the tree and headed out a little before dark. In the quickly dimming light, the colorful surroundings turned to a single shade of dark gray. Before long, everything began to look the same.

I had been in too big a hurry to mark a departure trail with my blaze-orange plastic ribbon when I entered the woods—a major mistake. I had depended on my memory of a specific oak, a rotting stump, and sheer luck to get me back to what would become my home base in the yard of the old Rodney house. Worse, when I dug for my flashlight and turned it on, I realized the little drum-playing bunny on the battery commercial had finally expired. I just knew I shoved those extra AA batteries in my pocket, but where were they?

After what seemed to be at least a half a lifetime of wandering about in a forest that had become as dark as the inside of a collapsed coal mine, I had to admit the inevitable to myself. *I'm lost!* Lost with no idea which ditch to follow, which tree I had noted while going in, or which way I needed to turn. I felt more alone than ever before. I can't count the times I said to myself, *If I could just find that oak tree, I'd get out of here tonight.* Somehow it was comforting to repeat the words.

In the available light of a half-moon that seemed to magically appear, I found a rock that hung over a low, mossy cliff. I looked at my watch and knew what I had to do. Thankfully, the temperature was tolerable as I prepared to spend a cool night in the forest. After making sure no other critters were bedded beneath the rocky overhang, I crawled under it, curled up, and hunkered down for the night.

With a half-humorous tone, I whispered to myself, "Maybe that Rodney boy who never found his way out of here will come wandering by and lead me back to his old house." It was an eerie wish, but I was desperate.

The night turned a little chillier than I expected. As I wrapped my arms around my chest and worked at staying warm, I realized that the darkness seemed deeper. I felt a growing fear of the unseen. It helped to talk to myself. "You can't let fear get the best of you. It can kill you like a deadly poison; it can invade your good sense and cause you to do crazy things, like start wandering around aimlessly. Just stay put, stupid."

After only a few seconds of silence I spoke to myself again, but with some deserved sarcasm. "Lost. What that meant to you yesterday, bubba, and what it means to you now are two totally different things."

Lost. I had time to think about the word that night, and I recalled how a pastor used it in his sermon at the funeral of a friend. He said, "When we say to one another, 'I'm so sorry you lost your loved one,' don't forget that nothing is lost when you know where it is."

What the pastor meant was if a person has trusted in Christ and has accepted His payment for sin, then when he leaves the forest of this life, there's no uncertainty about where he is going. If a person knows where they're going, and if their loved ones know it as well, then they're not lost. What a comfort.

I thought about the time I was lost—not physically, but spiritually. And I didn't really know it until I heard someone explain how my lostness began. It started in the Garden of Eden when Adam and Eve chose their independence over their innocence. Thanks to the deception of a clever serpent, the devil himself, they errantly decided that doing life their way was better than doing it God's way. God had given them a free will, and they used it to get lost. The bad news for me was that being a descendent of Adam and having inherited his sinful nature, my soul was just as lost and in need of being found. Enter the grace of God.

God, who is kind and compassionate, looked to His creation, and with a love that was so far-reaching that He was not willing that anyone would perish, He made a way for the lost to be found. That

Way would be His only begotten Son. The sinless Christ, perfect, blameless, and without failure, chose to come to the Rodney Hollers of this world to seek and save those who are lost.

I was definitely one of those lost wanderers. But blessed be the day when I heard this passage: "If you confess with your mouth the Lord Jesus and believe in your heart that God has raised Him from the dead, you will be saved" (Romans 10:9). I did my part, and God did His. I called out and confessed with my mouth, and He saved me. I was found.

In the shelter of the rock somewhere on the Rodney place where I hid in the darkness, I thought of the time I had made that decision, and a fresh flood of comfort washed over me. I knew that no matter how things ended in the pitch-black remotes of the wilderness I was in, I would be okay. If I lived through the night, I'd enjoy another day. If I died for some reason, I wouldn't die lost—at least not spiritually!

I couldn't believe it when the sky began to turn that familiar pale blue gray. I had hardly slept a wink the whole night. As the sun began to peek over the eastern horizon and offer some warmth, I wondered, *Did I just live a miracle? Amazing. But now, which way do I go?*

Suddenly, more questions hit me like a series of lightning strikes. *Don't you think it's time to pray and ask God for help? If He cared for you enough to keep you till morning, don't you think He can help you out of this hollow? If He died for you two thousand years ago, if He rose from the dead to give you life, do you not believe that He's alive now and cares about what happens to you this morning?* I knew the answers.

I bowed my head and prayed out loud, "O God, I know You hear me when I talk to You. You found me when I was lost in sin, and You know where I am right now. I couldn't find my own way out of a lost sinful condition, and I can't find my own way out of these woods. I need help. I need You. And by the way, I know I should have thought of this last night, but I didn't. Forgive me for that blunder too."

I sat for a while, feeling hungry enough to eat the rock I had slept under, and I tried to get my bearings from all my wanderings. As I scolded myself for the mess I was in, I heard a rustling in the leaves not fifty feet away. My thoughts ran wild. *Is it a bear, a bobcat, or worse yet, a pack of hungry coyotes that didn't get their fill overnight?* I slowly turned and peered from behind my rock fort that had become my hiding place. To my total surprise, a voice spoke.

"Hello, there! Seen anything?"

It was another hunter, but he didn't look like one of the Rodney boys—thankfully. He sported fresh camo, a gun with a stock that was obviously the latest state-of-the-art composite material, and boots that appeared to be barely broken in.

"You're the first and best thing I've seen this morning," I replied. "I've been here all night." I couldn't have been happier to know that another hunter was in the area nor more surprised by what he said next.

"We slept in the old Rodney house last night. It's not a hundred yards over this rise." Unbelievable! So close—yet so far away.

After a warm breakfast skillfully prepared on a Coleman stove in the old home place by a man who was a stranger only an hour earlier, I relayed the events of my failings. After listening to my pitiful confession, he offered, "If you would have just yelled, somebody here would have heard you."

What a fitting picture his words painted of the heart of every person in the darkened hollows of this life who realizes he or she is a lost hunter. Just a yell to heaven, and help will come. Is it time for you to call out? He made a promise to save the lost, and you can trust that He will come, even at this moment. You may be aware that you're as lost spiritually as I was physically in Rodney Holler that night. If so, this is my prayer for you.

Lord, for this one who is aware they are lost, let them sense Your love and recognize Your nearness in this hour. They may not realize You have led them to the place where they are right now. Would You give them the courage to call out to You in this moment? You care enough for them to make sure they're found, for You said You're not willing that they perish. Thank You for delivering them through the long night of lostness to the light of Your great love and grace. May their hearts be warmed and fed by the grace You have so freely given through Your sacrifice on the cross, Your burial, and Your resurrection.

In Your holy name, amen.

12

Back to the Blood

STEVE

I could not have been more certain that the crosshairs in the scope on my muzzleloader were in the right place on the tall-racked buck when I pulled the trigger. The cloud of smoke that poured from the barrel after the shot quickly thinned as the fifteen-mile-an-hour wind pushed it to my right. It allowed a fleeting glimpse of where the escaping deer left the open field and reentered the thicket. I made a mental note of the tree he skirted as he darted away.

I normally would have waited forty-five minutes to leave the stand and go to that spot, but I didn't think it was necessary. I felt very confident there'd be plenty of red splatter on the ground that would quickly lead me to my buck.

After searching at least ten minutes around the area where I last saw the deer, I found no evidence that my shot had connected. The only things I did find were some leaves and dark moist soil that had been freshly turned. I was sure they were signs made by the buck's hooves as he dug in deep and ran off.

I stood by the newly disturbed dirt, scanned ahead in all directions, and desperately hoped to see that familiar patch of white fur that covers the underside of a deceased deer's belly. Everywhere I looked there was nothing but dozens of leafless young saplings that stood in the brown, shin-high, winter-dead grass. My hopes faded. I had the emotion-draining suspicion that instead of following an easy blood trail I was about to enter the dreaded, signless, low-success-percentage process called "the body search."

I've learned to follow a procedure when I'm faced with a no-blood dilemma. First, wait. As the forty-five minutes crawled by, I replayed the shot in my head several times. *Did I jerk the gun when the hammer fell? Did I see the deer move just before the shot? Was there something between the buck and me that could have blocked the bullet?* I came up with negatives to all those questions. But then I remembered one detail that bothered me. Distance.

When daylight had come that morning, I had used my range finder to mentally place markers at 100 and 150 yards in each direction around me. Where the buck exited the thicket and walked into the field appeared to be about 100 yards away—or was it? The doubt didn't feel good.

I went back to the spot where the buck was standing when I took the shot, and using my range finder again, I checked the distance. Oh no! That's when I realized I had messed up. I should have adjusted for a longer shot. As a result, my 245-grain bullet likely fell too far and hit the target too low. What to do? There was only one answer, and I said it with a determined whisper. "Keep searching— be sure." The deer deserved the respect of my full commitment to finding him.

When it came time to resume the search, I went back to the upturned dirt I had marked with a small length of pink ribbon and once more scanned the area. At this point I started trying to see the area as a deer might see it. I looked for obvious deer trails, natural passages through the thicket, and obstructions (fallen trees or tangled vines) that would funnel deer toward a certain path. I saw all those features and knew I had only one choice. I would check each and every travel route I could see from where I stood.

I chose to search the most used and obvious trail first and slowly walked it, all the while carefully eyeing the ground and tall grass stems for blood spill. I can't tell you how high my heart leaped when, within twenty yards, I found a few drops of blood on a clump of leaves. I dropped to one knee and examined it closely for gut debris. It seemed clear of any evidence that would indicate a belly wound. I was relieved. The problem was, there wasn't much of it.

I marked the find with another piece of pink ribbon and walked forward down the trail. As emotionally high as I had been two minutes earlier, I was just that low after another twenty yards. Not another drop was found. I tried twenty more yards and got the same sad result. I stopped and did another visual, 360-degree scan, this time with and without binoculars. No downed deer in sight.

My shoulders drooped as I fought the demons of defeat. Not willing to give in, I knew there was only one thing I could do. It's a tactic every seasoned deer hunter turns to when a blood trail goes dry. Using my own voice of experience, I said it out loud: "It's time to go back to the blood."

I turned on my heels and headed back to the second pink marker. Seeing the bright red drops again brought back some hope. I again put on my whitetail cap and studied the thicket in front of me. *If I were a deer, what direction would I go from here?* When I saw what appeared to be a small depression where the buck might feel safe, I headed that way. As I passed through a break in some vines my heart leaped again. Blood! Not much—but it was blood.

As I tore off another three-inch patch of pink ribbon to temporarily attach to a vine at about waist level, I scanned the area ahead for a body. It's hard to say how much I longed for the search to end right then and there. All it would have taken was to spot some white underbelly, a tuft of snow-white hair on a tail, or the distinct, light beige color of antlers glowing in the shadows. But it didn't happen.

Regretting that the search had to continue, I slowly went ahead on the trail the deer appeared to be following. After another fifty yards—nothing. Another twenty-five yards—nothing. Once more I said, "Okay...back to the blood!"

It's hard telling how much cash I would give to be able to say that on that day my commitment to the buck was rewarded by finding more blood that eventually led me to him, but unfortunately it's not the report I can offer. To be honest, it's a painful thing to admit that after at least four hours of searching in the morning and another long attempt in the afternoon, I left the hunt empty-handed.

When unexpected and unwanted things like a lost deer happen while I'm hunting, I always try to review the details of it in order to glean something good and redeemable from the experience. In the case of the unrecovered buck, something of value did come of it— besides learning a big lesson about using my range finder. It was stored in my cell phone. Let me explain.

When I left the second discovery of blood and walked ahead to search for a third, only to find nothing more, what happened next stopped me in my tracks. As I mumbled, "Okay...back to the blood," I instantly left the hunter mode and for a moment entered the songwriter mode. It hit me like a ton of guitar picks that I had just stumbled onto a song idea worth writing down. Before I took another step I dug into my jacket pocket for my phone, pulled up my Notes app, and typed in, "Back to the Blood."

It would be a few days after licking my emotional wound for having injured a deer and not recovering it that I could mentally revisit the song idea. Using the very fresh imagery drawn from the hunt, I dove into the writing of the lyric. A couple of hours later it was finished, and when I read it aloud I thought, *I know that buck will never realize what his woe has yielded, but I wish I could tell him. Maybe it would ease the hurt a bit knowing that his pain was not wasted and that his blood was not shed in vain.*

BACK TO THE BLOOD

As I follow the Lord on the narrow road
Sometimes the cares of this life fall like a cloud around my soul
And steal His love from my sight
But when I need my hope renewed, faith has taught me
    what to do

I go back to the blood
Up to the place there on that hilltop
Where His red drops of grace fell to the ground
And gave me a sign that I am His and He is mine
I go back to the blood

Somehow the accuser knows when I'm weak
That's when he comes and whispers to me
Tells me I'm hopeless, redemption has failed
But that's when I follow that crimson trail
I go back to the blood[5]

> In Him we have redemption through His blood, the forgiveness of our trespasses, according to the riches of His grace (Ephesians 1:7 NASB).

13

The View Is Better from Up Here

DON

I'm glad I've lived long enough to get two important views of life. Each of them has helped me greatly, and each was shown to me by a very effective teacher.

In grade school (a millennia ago it seems), one of my teachers illustrated the meaning of the word *perspective* by requiring each of her students to take a turn sitting on the floor of the classroom and observing while others went about their normal activities. I was amazed as I watched the room from knee-high level. What would normally have been routine became a view of the world I had never seen before. My environment became a maze of legs, long britches, and dirty tennis shoes with untied strings.

My teacher may not have known what an impact the unusual activity would have on my life. Spending just a little time living three feet below everyone else helped me better understand what it means to feel humbled, to feel intimidated by those who tower over me in stature and power. Also, the memory of sitting on the floor still helps me empathize with anyone who feels envious of what others have. I even felt pity for pet dogs and cats that always have to look up at their world.

Years later, another teacher showed me another important perspective of my world. The other teacher is not a well-dressed, well-educated lady. Instead, it's an activity I discovered I liked to do, and it has given me the opposite point of reference in regard to life. It's deer hunting in a tree stand.

For me, climbing up into an elevated stand is not just a chance to conceal myself from the highly trained eyes of a whitetail. It provides more than just a better view of the beautiful creeks and picturesque clearings that grace my hunting grounds. There's a perspective of the world from up there that has literally changed the core of my character. I'm able to see things I've never noticed before.

One of the most memorable insights came one morning while I was gazing down at the woods from eighteen feet up. The leafy forest floor looked very much the same as far as I could see. However, when I took the time to look carefully among the layers of fallen leaves, I started seeing movement I hadn't noticed before.

There among the various shades of brown, I saw a mouse scampering from one hiding place to another. Chipmunks were doing the same, and insects crawled over and under the leaves. It was a busy place, and none of its inhabitants knew I was looking down on their activity with great interest.

In that moment, I got a hint of a God's-eye view of the world I live in. My wife, Doris, illustrated this perspective when we were on a flight and beginning to descend for a landing. She looked out the small, square window and asked, "Do you think this is the way God views the world?"

Her question captured my imagination. Quickly, I leaned across her lap and looked earthward. I saw an amazing view, one I normally would have ignored. It was an exceptionally clear day, and we seemed to be seeing everything below us in full HD. There were beautiful, lush, green fields. Others were freshly plowed, and some were surrounded by fencerows that made them appear to be little squares on a checkerboard. Dotting the landscape were small communities. I could see entire towns from our lofty perspective.

No, I couldn't tell which houses were fully built and which were unfinished, which ones were run down and which were well groomed. Each village was just a collection of neighborhoods, shopping centers, and streets. That was my view. But in response to my wife asking if I thought God sees it that way, I answered, "I think we both know that God goes deeper; He looks closer. He doesn't deal with generalities like we humans tend to do. He sees each one of us specifically and clearly. He knows us by name. None of us is a mere dot on the map to Him."

God's detailed view of each of us is well illustrated by what I saw one day while sitting in my climber at the edge of a large field. I watched a group of deer as they filed out of the timber and into the openness of a grassy corner. One, two, three, four…I finally counted fifteen in all. They were all ladies.

At first glance, each one was like the other. They all had similar features and generally the same actions. However, as I looked through my binoculars, I began to see them as individuals and not as a group. One had an unusual white spot on her lower left leg, another had a spot of dark hair on her back, and yet another had a split left ear. Amazingly, each doe had a unique, identifiable feature that separated her from the others.

A closer examination also revealed different actions and responses to what was going on around them. Some ate while others watched. Some just wandered away as if they had no concern for their safety. Some, apparently full from grazing, slowly laid down for a short siesta.

Just like that herd of does, when a group of humans is seen from a distance, we appear to look the same. Granted, we have different faces, different voices, different gaits, and different fingerprints, but for the most part, what we see in each other looks generally similar. But that's our view only.

God looks from a higher stand through very strong divine binoculars. He sees not only our individual forms and faces but also the inner recesses of our hearts. He sees the real person, the one behind the mask. He sees the individual underneath the emotional wounds, the weariness, the aimless wandering, and the facade of success. He sees it all.

According to His own Word, He knows even the "thoughts and intentions of the heart" (Hebrews 4:12 NASB). Can you imagine it? Every emotion, every memory, every plan is an open book to Him. God doesn't just see the communities and fields as I would see them from a 747. Rather, He peers behind every door of every house to see every soul. It's unimaginable but true. God sees you as a unique and private creation. He said, "Before I formed you in the womb I knew you; before you were born I sanctified you; I ordained you" (Jeremiah 1:5).

It's absolutely incredible to realize that He who formed the universe and all that is in it brought each of us into being by His own choice and called each of us to be a special, one-of-a-kind inhabitant of the cosmos. And then, as they say, He broke the mold. We see the herd, but God sees the hurt. Others can look only into our eyes, but God looks into our souls. And this same God, who numbered every hair on our heads, has a divine destiny planned for each and every life. "'I know the plans I have for you,' declares the LORD, 'plans to prosper you and not to harm you, plans to give you hope and a future'" (Jeremiah 29:11 NIV).

Perhaps the next time you make the climb into a tree stand and take your seat above the world, you will be reminded that while your vantage point gives you a good view of your surroundings, God is even higher above you (and much higher than all those kids who towered over me while I was sitting on the classroom floor). It's a humbling thought when you realize how incredibly clearly He views your life.

Actually, knowing that you are not hidden from His sight can bring you comfort. However, if you feel a little uncomfortable knowing He can see you so well, maybe it's time you and God had a talk while you're in the stand. After all, it's a place where you may feel a little closer to Him. If you do, I think you'll agree that when you begin to see life from God's stand, you'll be able to say, "The view is better from up here."

14

Ordered Steps

STEVE

I've had some strange things happen to me while deer hunting. Currently, this one ranks at the top of the "Say what?" list.

I had already changed into my camo and was standing in the predawn darkness outside my truck, checking emails on my phone, when I heard gravel popping under some tires. My friend was arriving to meet up for our morning deer hunt. Who else would be crazy enough to be awake at such a brutally early hour to voluntarily sit in twenty-five-degree December weather?

When he made the turn off the gravel and onto the logging road where I waited for him, his powerful high beams lit up the area as if it were a movie set. We had lights—all we needed were cameras and especially some action.

After loading our .270s and making sure our walkie-talkies were fully charged, we strategized our hunt. He would go to the far end of the third of three, long narrow fields and take a stand on the left side of the hollow at a place that the deer favored for crossing. I would start with him, but after about a hundred and fifty yards, I'd peel off and head up the hill on the right to an overlook where I could monitor the middle section of the first of the three fields.

We agreed that we'd stay on our stand until around nine o'clock. If neither of us had fired a shot by then, I would make a move since the wind would be in my face. The plan was for me to stay on the right side of the long hollow, where there was a lot of cover for the deer to bed, and I'd use the wind advantage as I walked through it. Our hope was that if I jumped any deer, they would work their way through the thicket ahead of me and then drop down the hill, right where my buddy would be waiting.

After nearly three hours of sitting in the cold and seeing nothing but squirrels and crows, I was very glad to stand up and start walking. I radioed my friend and said, "No action here. I'm about to be on the move. It'll take me at least thirty minutes to get to where I'll be above you on the opposite side of the hollow. I'll buzz you on the way."

He confirmed my announcement, and I began what was basically a one-man drive. It's not a high-percentage tactic, but the lay of the land and the fact that the right side of the hollow was a popular daytime hiding place for the local deer made the attempt worthwhile. I was not prepared for what was about to happen.

I got about halfway down the hollow, moving only a few yards at a time before stopping to listen. After going a little farther I radioed my friend to give him a progress report and to ask, "Seen anything yet?"

"Nope. All quiet here. The sun is feeling really good. I bet you're glad to be mobile!"

"Oh, yeah! I'm thawed out now. It feels good. I haven't stirred up any deer, but there's plenty of hillside left to cover. I'll keep pressin' on."

I got within about four hundred yards of the spot where I'd be right across the field and above my friend. By that time I had moved a little further up the hillside to a flat nearly at the top of the ridge. I walked ahead a little farther and stopped. Facing the place where I knew my drive would end, I listened for the telltale sound of deer running ahead of me. It was quiet. That's when I heard a voice in my head as real as if my friend were standing beside me speaking.

"Walk straight ahead. Don't waver to the left or right."

That was weird. I stood for a moment and looked around to make sure I was alone. About ten seconds passed, and feeling a bit bewildered, I just shook my head and whispered to myself, "Hmm…what are you gonna do with that, dude?" I wasn't sure.

I've had quiet thoughts before while deer hunting. *I should hunt the creek stand this morning instead of the ridge*, or *Don't go to the stand on the east side of the farm; go to the west side*, or *Use that tree instead of the other one for your climber*.

Conversations with myself like these were common. I suspect most hunters have had them too. But the instructions I heard that morning seemed different—very specific and, I confess, rather spooky. But half a minute later I thought, *What do I have to lose? I may as well give it a try.*

When I took a few steps forward, a mix of questions stopped me. *Am I listening to some sort of voice that's directing me into a death trap? Or is this a lesson about hearing God? Am I simply losing it? Have I hunted too long? What is this I'm doing?*

As probing and sobering as the unanswerable questions were, they didn't keep me from continuing to walk straight ahead as suggested. I stepped slowly, wondering if what I was doing was the right thing, all the while scanning the thicket for movement. A minute later, I felt inexplicably safe. After all, doing what I was doing was totally logical. If I stayed the course, I knew I would arrive exactly where I had planned to end the walk.

But then, about fifty yards from that predetermined spot, I heard another whisper. I stopped.

"Go to that tree just ahead and be prepared to shoot." Weird again.

There were lots of trees in front of me, but the one directly in my path was a young, slick-bark alder. When I took my first step toward it, the sound of my friend's rifle shot coming from the field edge below me seemed to shake the ground. Every muscle in my body tensed up with the blast. I instantly assumed I had unknowingly jumped a deer or two and they did exactly what we thought they'd do.

The field was about a hundred yards down the hill, and I hurried to the alder, rested my gun on the right side of the trunk and waited. Experience had taught me that as a reaction to my buddy's shot, the deer might turn and come back up the hill and maybe into the area where I waited. Sure enough, less than a minute later, here came two deer that seemed nervous as they sneaked through the timber. They were both does, my family's venison of choice.

As I took aim I was actually thinking about how amazing it was that I ended up at the tree where I stood. It felt surreal. When I fired my .270, the lead deer fell where it had stopped about twenty-five yards away. Twenty seconds later my walkie-talkie buzzed in my pocket.

"Was that you that shot?"

"Yes, it was. I think you took a shot too. Right?"

"I did. There's a doe on the ground on the other side of the field from me at the bottom of the hill you're on. You got one down?"

"I do. A doe. Looks like it's a double day for us. Can't believe our one-man drive worked so well!"

"Amen. Speaking of work, time to break out the knives. I'll come up and help you drag yours down to the field."

I knew my friend would be glad to hear me say, "No bother. It's downhill from here. I'll see you in a little bit. And hey…do I ever have a weird thing to tell you!"

As we cleaned our bloodied knives in the creek at the bottom of the hill, I told my friend about hearing the specific instructions up on the hillside and how they seemed to contribute to the outcome of our hunt. He looked at me as if he were worried about me. I didn't blame him. I was a little worried about me too.

For several days, I pondered what had happened and was troubled that I didn't have a clear explanation for hearing such precise instructions. I even prayed and asked the Lord to forgive me if I had listened to a voice from the dark side. I definitely didn't want to open the door of my heart to anyone or anything evil. I also asked Him to show me something good from the experience—and I believe He did.

There are two familiar verses in the Psalms that address the divine ordering of a man's steps. One is a promise, and the other is a prayer.

- "The steps of a good man are ordered by the LORD,
  And He delights in his way" (37:23).

- "Direct my footsteps according to your word;
  let no sin rule over me" (119:133 NIV).

When I read these verses, I sensed a comfort in my soul regarding the strange encounter in that long hollow. I apparently had been given a lesson tailor-made for a hunter about how to follow God's plan for my trail. First I need to trust that He will keep His promise to plan my steps through the woods of this life. Then I can call on Him to lead me by speaking to my heart through His Word.

God knows I want to hear Him say to my heart, *Go this way, stop, wait, speak, be still, stand firm*, or anything else He wants me to hear. I know if I listen to Him and take the steps He has ordered for me, life will go better for me. And how thankful I am that my resolve to do so was strengthened on that cold day on a hunter's hillside.

> Whether you turn to the right or to the left, your ears will hear a voice behind you, saying, "This is the way; walk in it" (Isaiah 30:12 NIV).

15

What I Saw

DON

For many years prior to being blessed with my own little piece of hunting real estate, I was limited to pursuing whitetail on property owned by the government. The problem I dealt with was that the public land was much more public than I preferred.

I'm aware that everyone had as much right to be there as I did, but it was so frustrating to make the effort to get on a stand before daylight only to hear the sound of a gas-powered four-wheeler putt-putting along a distant ridge, carrying someone into the area. Or at first light I'd catch a glimpse of blaze orange moving through the woods. Though whoever it was would take a stand somewhere out of view, it was discouraging just to know they were in the vicinity.

But as unwanted as the presence of others can be, I will admit that a couple of good things have come from it.

Some of my best deer-hunting action has occurred when hunters in a public area decided it was time to get up and go before I did. They may have been restless or hungry for lunch, or they may have planned on meeting someone. Regardless of their intentions, early leavers have worked on my behalf at times as they exited the woods. The noisy scrape of their boots across logs they *almost* stepped over, the cracking of branches, the tromping through crisp fallen leaves, and the cell-phone conversations have pushed escaping critters right by me on more than one occasion.

Then, in the early afternoon, these same fidgety folks often re-entered the woods and once again unwittingly triggered some action by startling a group of whitetail that didn't see me in my stand as they snuck away. I confess that when it resulted in taking a shot, it was satisfying to think that the returning hunters heard the booming report of my big-caliber gun. I knew they couldn't hear me thank them for helping me fill a tag, but I did!

The other benefit that has come from the unwanted dilemma of having other hunters in my area was how it helped me learn to be a nicer person. To explain, on more than one occasion I would hear the snap of a twig or crunching of leaves behind me and I'd nervously but excitedly prepare for a confrontation with what sounded like a heavy-bodied, Boone and Crockett–sized trophy. Then, like a failed rocket that dropped back on the launch pad, my hopes would come crashing down as I'd turn to see a two-legged, blaze-orange-clad human intruder strolling my way. That's when I'd sometimes let my mischievous side take over. I would wait until they were below me and make sure my voice was loud enough to be heard over their walking as I delivered an unhappy sounding, "Hello?" Saying it in question mode was intentional. I wanted whoever they were to be shocked and know that I was questioning their presence.

There's a certain gratification I'd feel when I spoke and the unsuspecting invader gave an instant jerk of the body, twisting of the head, and a backward step. My other favorite reaction was hearing their high-pitched, infant-like, frightened whine when they heard my voice. Mission accomplished.

In almost every instance when I'd successfully startle an unwelcomed guest with my antic, they wanted to start a conversation. Of course, it wasn't usually a humble, "Oh man, I'm so sorry, I had no idea you were already in these woods. I'll sneak out and let you get back to hunting." No, that's not what they'd say. Instead, their first sentence was typically a two-word question.

"Seen anything?"

In an attempt to be vague enough not to report about the bruiser buck I might have spotted in the area, I would normally give some sort of impish answer, like "They're around. Must be present to win!"

While my answer was true and served me well in sending a wanderer on his way without too much information, I knew it sounded rude and unfriendly. Eventually, my intentional display of bad manners began to gnaw at me, and I came to the realization that I needed a nonhostile answer to their, "See anything?" Thankfully, I found something to say that helped me feel better about myself. I just hope it helped those who heard it to feel better too.

The idea came to me one day in early bow season when I stayed out from dawn till dark. Spending that much time in the stand gave me a chance to observe a constant show of the Creator's awesomeness. By the end of the hunt, I had a game bag full of answers to give the next hunter who would invade my space.

To name a few of the things I saw, I'll start with the clear, predawn sky filled with innumerable stars shining out of the deep blackness. Their countless presence serves as an incredible reminder of God's promise to Abraham ages ago in a distant land: "I will make your descendants multiply as the stars of heaven" (Genesis

26:4). Knowing from biblical history that God kept His word and did indeed bless Abraham the way He said He would made the pre-sunrise scene even more inspiring.

Among the vast host of white dots was a light that seemed bigger than all the rest. Its brilliance and position far beyond our sun and moon made me wonder if it was the one shining star that led the wise men to a child who was and is the Savior of the world. Its impressive existence tells me that the heavens in all their beauty really do faithfully declare His glory.

I had already seen some amazing things before the sun peeked across the distant horizon in the east. There was more to come. A blazing red sphere of light gradually began to appear and warm my chilling flesh as I sat in the brisk morning air. What an awesome reminder that in the rising of the sun there's life, but as brilliant as it is, it's a mere symbol of the Light of the World, who is now seated at the right hand of God, praying for those He calls His own.

With the arrival of the bright daylight and the intensely colorful scenes of nature that came with it, I began to see why God would cancel nighttime in eternity. Surely it's because everything He has prepared for the eyes of His followers is so awesome, He doesn't want anyone to miss a single part of it! How amazing to think that there will be no threat of darkness in heaven—only eternal day. Wow!

In every green blade of grass on the ground below me, in the golden morning sunshine that sliced through the trees, in the gray mist suspended over the lake, and in the deep red of the cardinal, I saw colorful evidence of the work of eternal hands.

In the quietness of the midday I watched as things all around me seemed to go into nap mode. I joined in, and after a few minutes of some of the sweetest sleep known to man, I awoke with a renewed appreciation for God's brand of peace, the kind that passes all understanding.

In the late afternoon I watched as wildlife movement began to happen again all around me. Everything with legs seemed to begin feeding on nuts while creatures with feathers flew in to munch on the small bugs that lived and crawled on the tree bark. What a glorious sight to behold!

Then, as if it had been only a moment since sunrise, a sphere of white began to usher in the evening. I quietly observed the descending sun leaving its mark on a rising moon and thought, *Lord, only You can create a wonder like that!*

Before I headed home, I looked around and realized that the world I had watched throughout the day was just one tiny piece of a much larger, universal picture. As the cooler breeze of the late evening swept across my cheeks, I thought to myself, *No truer words have been written than these: "Eye has not seen, nor ear heard, nor have entered into the heart of man the things which God has prepared for those who love Him"* (1 Corinthians 2:9). *If I lived a million lifetimes, I would never see it all!*

I didn't take a shot at anything on that hunt, but I was not disappointed by it. What could be better than a dawn-to-dusk look at God's art? That's when I decided what my answer would be from then on if a startled, wide-eyed intruder asked, "Seen anything?"

I'd smile and say, "Yes—are you free for a couple of hours?"

WHAT I SAW

I saw a picture today, not one hanging in a studio or posted in
   a museum;
One that was a particular moment no one will ever behold
   but me.
Not one wandering soul will ever see that leaf fall and hit the
   ground again,

Not in a million lifetimes.

No life before or after me will ever feel the joy of this warm
moment as a beautiful bird perched on a limb just inches
from my head and sang a song just for me.

No other tongue can ever tell the story of watching the doe rise
on her hind legs, as if to greet me, and then munch a meal
from the leaves below my stand.

Pen can never write of the beauty when a small fawn stretched
to touch its nose to her mother as if to kiss her and say,
"Thanks for the joy of being with you this morning."

Though many may experience these joys, these moments are
mine—made just for me.

What love, what grace, that God would take the time, create
the gift, and present it to me as an awesome moment of
creation.

And then, somehow, on the canvas of my heart He paints
a picture, one man staring into the face of another
hanging on a cross and hearing a voice that simply says,
"It is finished, just for you, it is finished!"

I saw the beauty,

I saw the wonder,

I saw creation,

I saw Calvary, just for me.

Have you seen it?[6]

16
He's Not There

STEVE

I sat down on the cushion of my ladder stand and began the wait for first light. Sunrise seemed to take longer than normal that morning. The lingering darkness made me think someone had pushed the cosmic pause button on the earth's rotation. Finally, as if the resume button was pressed, daybreak came. It was time to start deer hunting.

My stand leaned securely against a tall, stout oak at the edge of a field. I had pruned the limbs before the new season started, so I had two really good shooting lanes but enough foliage on the remaining branches to conceal my presence.

The tall oak towered over me like a giant umbrella, and the acorns fell like rain from its branches. In fact, there were so many nuts on the ground that I had to watch where I stepped to keep the shells from noisily cracking under my boots. With such an abundant food source beneath me, my hopes for seeing deer were high, and it didn't take long for those hopes to be met.

About twenty minutes after sunrise I looked across the field and spotted a really nice buck. He had exited the woods and then stopped, as they always seem to do, to check his surroundings. He then began to walk to my side of the field. The problem was that by then he was about seventy-five yards downrange and out of my view.

Fifteen minutes passed, and I hadn't seen him again, so I assumed that once he got to the edge of the woods he decided to walk straight into them and head up the hillside. Happily, I was wrong. About the time I thought he had eluded me, he came wandering down the edge of the field right toward my stand. I thought, *If he keeps coming, he'll be just twelve yards away through the first shooting lane.* That's exactly what happened.

To avoid any chance of being seen when he walked in close, I chose not to stand up for the shot. Instead, I leaned forward, turned slightly to the right with my upper body, and pulled the compound string back with just a little extra effort. I was at full draw in plenty of time to press the release trigger when he got to the opening. When the arrow left the string, there was no doubt in my mind it would find its mark.

The buck, an eight point, kicked (as deer often do when struck by an arrow), turned more than ninety degrees to the right, and ran back across the field to where he had entered it a half hour earlier. He stopped just inside the woods, stood there for maybe ten seconds, and then toppled over. The deal was done, and I pounded my leg to release the glorious tension.

Feeling sure it was okay to head on over to the deceased deer, I gathered my gear and climbed down. As I walked toward the buck, I congratulated myself for a well-planned, successful hunt. I like spending as much time as I can in the woods, so I wished it would have lasted longer into the morning, but I knew I wouldn't change what had just happened. Chances like that didn't come along every day.

I had mentally noted where the deer fell and easily found the light gray tree that marked the spot. When I got close to it I fully expected to see the heavy body of the deer lying there, but I didn't. All I could think was, *He's not there. Where'd he go?*

I took five more steps toward the spot I had marked and saw a significant pool of blood on the leaf-covered ground but no buck. I started to back out and head to the truck before returning to locate the deer, but before I did, I decided to take a few more steps inside the timber to take a look. I'm glad I did. The eight-pointer had somehow found the strength to get up and move. He was lying lifeless about forty yards away.

Even now as I recall the story of the hunt, one particular scene moves me to the very core of my soul. It's my reaction when I got to the place where I assumed he'd be lying dead, only to face the surprise of his absence. *He's not there!* The reason I'm affected by that specific detail is that my words are exactly what my mother said to me in reference to my late dad. He was her love of sixty-nine years. Here's a lyrical version of the unforgettable memory.

HE'S NOT THERE

Daddy died a year ago
He's buried on a hill
Just a few miles down the road
From his old home in Chapmanville
Mama's living by herself
I called her just today

It was good to hear she's doing well
She's never been back to the grave
I said, "Mom, don't you think it's time
I'll come home and take you there, I wouldn't mind"
That's when Mama said

"He's not there, oh, he's not there
His name is on that stone I know
But he's not there
Through eyes of faith I see him now
In heaven's land so fair
For you I'll go, but child I know
He's not there"

She said, "God knows how I miss that man
I'd love to see his smile
And feel the tender in his hands
And walk with him awhile
If I could go and hear him say
'Could I have this dance?'
I'd be there every day
I wouldn't want to miss that chance
All I have is our sweet memories
But they're not buried on that hillside
They live inside of me"

"He's not there, oh, he's not there
His name is on that stone I know

But he's not there
Through eyes of faith I see him now
In heaven's land so fair
For you I'll go, but child I know
He's not there"[7]

All of us have loved ones who have passed from this life to the next. Those who claimed redemption through Christ leave us with great hope, just as my dad did for my mom, my sister and me, and our families. My goal is to do the same for those I love so that when I'm gone and they think of my burial place, they can find comfort in saying, "He's not there!" I hope you have the same goal.

> Jesus said to her, "I am the resurrection and the life. He who believes in Me, though he may die, he shall live" (John 11:25).

17

How to Kill a Hunter

DON

Many years ago I believed that deer hunting season was a contest, and the trophy went to the hunter who could claim the most points. I was wrong, but I didn't realize I needed an attitude adjustment. Did I want to harvest a magnificent animal? You bet I did. But the more important question was, can I rightly handle the pride that comes with a monster buck? A deer I respectfully refer to as Mr. Boss provided the answer and a timely dose of reality.

Mr. Boss earned his title from his many years of rubbing cedars nearly the size of telephone poles and making scrapes that looked more like dry ponds. Of the bucks that roamed the three hundred acres of deer heaven that our group hunted, the Boss was the most desired specimen among them. All of us dreamed of putting him in our sights.

The sign Mr. Boss left on the property became easily recognizable. It was always exciting during preseason scouting for one of us to see it and announce to the band of hunting brothers, "I saw his sign! He's still here—he survived last season!" The excitement, the anticipation, the rise in our body temperature brought a welcome fever that could be treated only with the medicine of opening morning.

I would immediately start searching for the perfect place to take a stand along a trail that Mr. Boss favored in order to gain the better ambush advantage over the rest of the guys. I was driven by the thought, *If I could be the shooter when the big boy walks by, I'll be the champion.* Winning was everything.

The first day of season finally arrived, and our group dispersed into the woods before dawn. As I settled into my chosen stand site, the fog rose off the small pond at the edge of the clearing I planned to watch. I carefully placed my backpack to my side so it wouldn't be seen from any direction that Boss Man might approach. The tree I had chosen to sit at was on a small rise, and the extra height allowed a perfect 360-degree view of my surroundings.

I watched a few females slip in next to the pond and briefly drink from the clear pool. It was like seeing a reenactment of Psalm 42:1: "As the deer pants for the water brooks, so my soul pants for You, O God" (NASB). It made the heart of even a trophy-driven hunter like I was stop for a moment and feel the warmth of the scene...at least until I saw another doe bounce out of the woods into the edge of the small field.

Her behavior was familiar. It was the "come and catch me" dance a doe will do during mating season. When she abruptly stopped and turned to view the path she had taken out of the woods, I followed her line of vision back to the brush. In the pursuit of the "big rabbit," I've come to understand that when this scenario happens during rut, a boyfriend is more than likely close behind. I didn't even breathe as I waited to see why she was on the move.

When I glanced back again to the place where she exited the woods I saw what appeared to be a group of cedar limbs moving through the brush toward the frost-covered field. Suddenly, in full view, there he stood! He was the most beautiful whitetail I had ever seen. The stance he took with his massive dark body appeared to dare any other male to approach his sweetheart. What a sight to behold!

The next thing about him I noticed was his very swollen neck, which supported a set of antlers that resembled tree branches growing out of his head. And as I've been known to do when a beast of such stature appears, I broke the "don't utter a word" rule and whispered, "It's him! It's the Boss!"

My adrenalin immediately started flowing like water through a fireman's hose. My nerves felt as if they had been hooked up to a car battery as my arm and leg muscles began to quiver. Somehow, though, in the flurry of mind and body malfunction, my fingers still crawled to the safety and then onward to the trigger of the cannon that somehow raised itself to my shoulder.

I've never been one to hold back on praying in the midst of a hunting challenge, and that morning was no different. *God, give me the ability to do what I know to do. Help my body not to break apart and fall to the ground in small pieces.*

As always happens with a muzzleloader, smoke filled the air like London fog when the exploding powder pushed the hollow-point copper bullet out the barrel. I tried to look through it but couldn't. Not being able to see where Mr. Boss ran after the shot made me start to worry. I could feel an uneasy nausea deep in my stomach as I said to myself, *Surely I couldn't have missed. Surely!*

Finally, as if a veil lifted, I got a clear view of the wood line where he had stood. The doe he had followed was gone. There was nothing but silence as I thought, *Where did he enter the timber? Which way would he exit this scene?* Then, as if an unseen hand gripped my cheeks and moved my head slowly back and forth, I scanned the field on either side of where he had stood. My worry suddenly turned to unbridled joy.

Among the sparkling droplets of melting frost on the tall grass was an incredible sight. Like a little boy seeing his first bicycle under a Christmas tree, I was giddy when I saw a massive rack of pure white bone rising above the grass. "It's him!" I yelled to myself. "He's down!"

Approaching him as carefully as I could without shaking, I poked him in the eye with my reloaded muzzleloader to make sure of his demise. Then I started counting. One, two, three...all the way up to sixteen massive points! All were perfect and undamaged from his season of duels with other local brutes.

With a twenty-six inch spread, I was confident he was a record-book buck. "A wall mount for sure," I whispered to myself as I placed my small measuring tape back into my pocket. "I win." Then I imagined meeting up with the rest of the group and saying, *Guys, meet the champ.* I couldn't wait to see the envy in their eyes, and they weren't the only folks I hoped to impress.

Several months later when the taxidermist delivered the mount of Mr. Boss, I hung it above the mantle. Time and time again visitors viewed my harvest of the hills and said the one word I liked hearing most—"Wow!"

To be honest, it became quite a heady thing to have every hunter's dream on my wall and especially to be the envy of any novice who was beginning the journey of accomplishing a feat such as mine. It was a status I enjoyed...until one day I climbed a bit too high into the tree of triumph. It was from that dangerous height that I learned the hard way what God meant when He spoke of pride coming before destruction and a haughty spirit before a fall.

It happened when a very nice young man named Tim landed a job where I worked.

I found out Tim liked to hunt and had been doing it only a little while. He had spent the first couple of seasons learning all he could and trying hard to get his first deer, but it hadn't happened. When he asked for advice that would help him correct the mistakes keeping him from filling his first tag, I was happy to offer it. Then one early Saturday morning he connected with his first whitetail, and the one person he most wanted to tell was me.

I had just come in from a morning hunt and was standing in our kitchen enjoying a cup of Columbian java when I heard a truck turn down my driveway. If it had been another hunter coming to ask for permission to hunt on my domain, he would have been wasting his time. But that's not who it was.

As I went to our front-room window and peered out at the now parked vehicle, I recognized Tim's truck. He looked excited as he approached our front door. Before he knocked, I said out loud, "Aha, it's Tim! I bet he's gotten permission for me to hunt with him at that farm we've talked about. This could be a great day."

He seemed high-spirited as he stepped across our front porch. His loud, quick knock sounded as if he was anxious for me to open the door. When I did he grabbed me by my arm and nearly dragged me outside.

"I got one!" he said, "I got my first one, Don. Come and see it!"

Marching me to his trophy in back of his pickup, he pointed at it, shook me by the shoulder, and again verbalized his excitement. "There she is. Ain't she a beauty? She's my first! Whaddya think?"

I stood in silence for a moment as I looked at the pitiful, lifeless animal on the bed of his pickup. It looked more like a young collie than a deer. I thought to myself, *Poor kid. He needs to see what a real deer looks like.*

I attempted my best *Crocodile Dundee* imitation. "That's not a deer." Then I said, "Come inside and let me show you what a real deer looks like."

My young friend quietly walked behind me as we stepped into my home, turned the corner through the living room, and entered the area where Mr. Boss hung on the wall. I pointed up at the massive buck and spoke with a voice a little deeper than normal. "Now that's a deer, Tim. That's what you're lookin' for."

He stood for a few speechless moments, stared above the mantle, and finally broke the silence. His voice was a little subdued as he spoke.

"Man, that's a nice one." His shoulders drooped as he looked at me and said again, "Yessir, that's a really nice deer. Guess I better go and get mine checked in."

As he drove away, I grabbed my cup, took a sip of coffee, and thought to myself, *That'll give him something to dream about.*

The noise of the gravel popping under his truck tires was interrupted by my wife's voice. I was so caught up in the opportunity to school Tim in the art of real hunting that I hadn't noticed she had been sitting there when I escorted him into our den.

"Congratulations." Her tone sounded challenging.

I looked up at my sixteen-point and answered, "It is a great deer, isn't it?"

"That's not what I'm talking about," she said. "Congratulations on killing a young hunter."

"What?" Her statement didn't register at first, so I finished my question. "What are you talking about?" She slowly sat her coffee on the small table beside her chair and leaned forward.

"I assume that was Tim from your work, the young man you've been talking about?"

"Yep. He got his first deer and wanted to show it to me."

"That's what I gathered. I saw the two of you looking at it out there in his truck. He sure was excited."

"Yes, but I gave him something bigger to dream about today."

My wife is not one to mince words, but she's also not one to intentionally throw them out like barbs. She chose her words carefully and kindly as she assessed what she had just seen.

"Honey, when that young man came in our door today, you were his best chance of feeling the joy of a huge accomplishment. He wanted nothing from you but a handshake of congrats and some kudos. You didn't give it to him. He's hunted hard, dreamed of this moment, and picked the one person he thought would appreciate the result the most. And what did you give him? A bullet right through the center of his spirit. You killed him. Couldn't you see it in his face? You killed the joy and anticipation of sharing a great moment with you. Oh, you found the biggest deer, but you may have lost something much more valuable—a good friend."

I stood for a moment while my world fell in around me. My dear wife had helped me realize that my must-win attitude as a hunter had risen up and showed its ugly self. Sadly, I had taken the dagger of pride and plunged it deep into my own soul—and Tim's as well. The words came from deep within as I said, "O Lord, what have I done?"

Tim and I continued to work together at our job. We talked sometimes and even mentioned hunting every now and then. However, it wasn't the same with us. It seemed that my ego had done too much damage. I asked God to forgive me, and I know He did, but whenever I'd see Tim walk by and head to his workstation, I imagined how he felt that day at my house when I shot a hole in his soul. The memory brought the worst kind of regret—the kind that comes from doing something I knew I could have done differently.

Several times I offered my place to Tim to hunt, but he never did take me up on it. I can't say I blame him. Sometimes when I look at the buck over the mantle, I think of him and what a reckless thing I said. I think of my error especially during deer season. When I do, the same prayer crosses my heart. *Lord, if Tim is in the woods right now, would You send a Boss buck his way? If it's okay with You, would You give him his heart's desire as a hunter? And if You grant it, please encourage him to come by and share his success story with me. I'd be so thankful for the chance to heal an old and awful wound. Amen.*

18

Close Call

STEVE

It would be better if this story could not be told.

The ground was frozen and hard because of the three consecutive twenty-degree days in the area. The grass under the light dusting of snow that covered the hillside was crunchy and noisy, but that wouldn't be a problem for the rabbit hunters who had gathered at the farm. They knew that on a frigid day the cottontails would sit tight in the brush as long as they could before darting out ahead of any incoming intruders.

The four men didn't yet have the advantage of the trio of beagles they had planned to use for jumping up the rabbits. The fifth guy who owned them had called early and said he was delayed and wouldn't be able to join them until almost noon. But that didn't stop the gang from getting started. Why waste the morning? They had a plan. They would be both hunters and dogs.

The briars and brush on the hillside were about waist high, so they decided they could do the hunt side by side about thirty yards apart. To be safe, they would move along slowly while keeping an eye on each other to make sure no one got too far out in front of the line. If someone jumped a rabbit, they agreed to yell loud and clear, "There he goes!" It would be the cue for the rest of the foursome to get ready to shoot—and of course to aim only forward of the group.

After draping themselves with the legal requirement of blaze orange on their coats and hats, the shotgun-toting team headed up the hill. The one with the youngest legs was sent to the top and took his position. Using him as the reference, the other three formed a straight line that stretched almost to the creek below.

With their guns loaded and fingers sitting just outside the trigger guards, the eldest among them said, "Let's do it!" At his command the men began to press forward through the belt-high thicket of stringy briars and tangled vines. At their feet were clumps of grassy growth that looked perfect for a rabbit's day home.

After about ten minutes of ripping through the briars that chewed like shark's teeth into their pants, the young guy hollered excitedly, "There he goes!"

Three seconds later the next man down the hill pulled his trigger and rolled a rabbit to its final resting place. After he retrieved the fluffy prize, the men realigned themselves and started the march again. Four shots and two cottontails later one of them said, "Hey, who needs beagles? This is working great!"

Once more they got a visual on each other, lined up, and began hunting, watching one another and the ground as they went. But then the brush got a little higher for several yards, and the guy on the bottom of the line unknowingly moved ahead of the group about ten yards, scanning the ground for places that looked like a temporary rabbit lair. That's when the next man above him yelled, "There he goes!"

At the bottom, the hunter looked up the hill and saw a flash of gray fur running directly at him. In the next instant he looked farther up the hill and saw something he didn't want to see. Through the tight network of briars and vines that draped the limbs of the shoulder-high saplings, he saw the distinct shape of a gun barrel against a background of blaze orange.

The hunt had worked well to that point with everyone keeping the safe line, so the hunter above him was sure it was okay to blast away at the rabbit. With his focus on the target zigzagging along the ground, he didn't see the blaze orange beyond it through the brush. He pulled the trigger of his shotgun.

The moment he heard the blast, the bottom hunter could do only one thing besides pray. As though everything suddenly moved into slow motion, he turned his gaze from the black hole of the shotgun barrel and twisted his face away. He could hear the BBs peppering the leaves and limbs around him. He didn't immediately feel the sting on his jaw as his head swirled backward, but he did feel the buckshot hitting his thick overalls and hat. He went to his knees.

Everyone above him heard the scary yell that followed the shot. "Oh man! I've been hit!" Within twenty seconds he was surrounded by a trio of friends whose hearts were beating fast from running and from fearing what they'd find.

As the downed hunter assessed his condition, he realized very quickly that he didn't hurt anywhere on his body. As he stood up to comfort his comrades with the good news about how he felt, he rubbed his bearded left jaw. That's when he felt the warm blood on his hand. He was afraid to ask, but he knew he had no choice.

He jutted his jaw and asked, "How bad is it?"

An older hunter made a quick examination and determined that the wound was not deep and appeared more like a two-and-a-half-inch scratch made by the claw of a cat. There didn't seem to be any penetration by the lead shot. Everyone simultaneously sighed with relief.

The bleeding was not excessive and soon stopped. Perhaps the cold air helped. The conversation for the next few minutes was filled mainly with apologies from the shooter, some onsite forgiveness, some sincere thanks to God that they weren't carrying a hunter off the hill, and some talk about the hunting method they used that started well but ended not so well.

They all agreed that the one good thing about where the incident happened was that the load of shot from the 12-gauge shell was slowed by the thick growth it went through. Otherwise, more than one pellet might have found the victim's face.

With three rabbits in the bag, the four grateful hunters decided to call it a morning and wait for the guy with the beagles to show up. Of course, on the way back to the vehicles they kicked the frost-covered grassy clumps with their boots in hopes of more action.

How do I know they did? Because I was in the group—and I was the one with the scratch on my jaw!

For the sake of anonymity for the guys, especially the unintentional shooter, I won't say who they were or where it happened. But I will say that many times through the years I've relived the moment when I stared into the dark eye of that 12-gauge. The words "There he goes" still echo in my mind along with the sound of a deafening boom and the instantaneous ticks and clicks made by the cluster of #5 shot hitting all around me.

I suppose it was instinct to quickly turn away from the blast...or did an angel spin me around? I won't know until the life beyond this one. But what I do know is that each remembrance of such a close call with disaster provides a new opportunity to credit God for the outcome. To credit anyone else, or anything such as luck, would simply be wrong. May God alone be praised.

19
How's the Weather Up There?

DON

It's strange how a specific memory can come to mind while I'm hunting. For example, one morning my thoughts went back about twenty years to a basketball game in the gym at my high school alma mater.

Three seconds to go, the score is tied, and the roar of the crowd in the bleachers is deafening. We have one chance to win. The ball won't go to a guard for an outside shot, nor will we try to get it to a forward and plow our way through the man-to-man defense for a layup. No time for that.

There's just one shot at victory and a short time to try it. The only real hope we have stands six feet six. He's in the middle of the pack of sweaty jerseys, short trunks, and beat-up Converse tennis shoes. His name is Dallas.

Who was Dallas? He was a senior who seemed as big to us as the city in Texas. He played center and was a full head above most others on the floor. He could leap above the basket from a standing jump and could always place the ball somewhere in the vicinity of the hoop—or at least draw a foul.

The inbound pass goes to Dallas, and with the rubbery thud of a couple of quick dribbles, he spins around to face the basket. The last-second shot he launches toward the glass backboard acts like it's looking for the orange metal ring. The home-team fans hold their breath. Finally, after a few heart-stopping bounces, it falls through at the buzzer. Game over—we win! Once again, our best chance on the floor, our mountain among the hills, gets the job done.

It was good to remember Dallas again. Who could forget him? With his height and long, lanky body, Dallas always stood out in the hallways of our school. Finding him was easy—we just looked over everyone else's head, or if he was seated, we looked for a cluster of girls, because he was handsome too.

Being a handsome and talented athlete in our little school had a downside for Dallas. All of us who looked up to him (literally!) wanted to be like him. Back then, some of us wanted what he had so bad, jealousy and envy quietly simmered in our souls. We knew we could never have what number 18 had, so some of us tried to bring him down to our size. To belittle him, we didn't target his good looks. Instead, Dallas got a lot of taunting about his height.

When he was walking to class, standing at his locker, or chatting with the head cheerleader in the hallway, one of us would walk by and ask, "Hey, Dallas, how's the weather up there?" We didn't think about how silly and overused the question was. All we were thinking was how much we hoped it would irritate and embarrass him. But Dallas would just grin and bear our verbal jabs without a trace of anger.

I'm not sure where he found the restraint to keep from spitting on the one who asked the question and saying, "It's raining up here!" But somehow he showed a lot of patience and managed to make it through his years in school without squashing any of his mockers under his size-twelve shoes (which we annoyingly referred to as his river barges). All of us underlings would have deserved to hear him say something like, "I'd make a joke about how short you are, but it would just go over your head!" But I never heard him say anything of the sort.

That day in the deer stand wouldn't be the last time I'd remember Dallas and his enviable stature. I thought of him again during a deer hunt in a mountainous western state. I was climbing a tall mountain, and about halfway up I thought, *I wonder what the weather's like up there?* With that familiar question came the mental image of Dallas's face. I thought again about how much I would have given back in high school to be able to stand on my tiptoes like he did and gather the net into my fingers, and how much I wished I'd been the "babe magnet" he was. But thanks to the passage of time and the maturity that comes with it, his physique and popularity no longer bothered me.

Thinking about Dallas without the distraction of jealousy opened my eyes to the fact that he had something more than a major inch advantage on those of us who badgered him with our juvenile comments. He was also taller in character, showing kindness in the face of unkindness and displaying patience when impatience would have been understandable. Where did he find the strength to refrain from retaliating against our tall jokes with justifiable jabs at our shortness? I know the answer.

Considering his gentle demeanor and the mercy he showed his tormenters, maybe it wouldn't be a surprise to know that his kindhearted personality was rooted in his faith in Christ. He was taught to love those who mistreated him and not to repay evil with evil or insult with insult. When I finally understood why Dallas was who he was, it helped me see that the only hope I had of being a person anyone would want to look up to was found in having a relationship with Jesus. Thankfully, I'm one of His followers now, and He alone has made me taller in character. I haven't attained the height I long for, but I pray often that God will make me a Dallas-size man of faith.

What a legacy that lanky lad left in my heart. I wondered how many other guys in our school eventually recalled Dallas with the same kind of affection and inspiration. How many of us could finally admit, just as I did, that our former teammate was someone worthy of imitating? Only God knows.

Where is number 18 now? Dallas graduated from high school and married the head cheerleader, and together they raised three beautiful children. His name still tops the list at our alma mater for points scored in a season.

With faith as his foundation, he went on to pastor a great church in southern Kentucky. That fine city is now richer for it, and heaven is too, because Dallas introduced many souls to the redemption Christ offers. His contributions of time, talent, and teaching were more priceless than gold to those he served. They would all agree that he literally and spiritually stood tall in the pulpit.

I was sad beyond words the day I heard that Dallas was diagnosed with a terminal cancer. He lived only a few weeks afterward. The good news is, before he went home to heaven, I was blessed to become best of friends with him. We spent a lot of time over the years climbing mountains and hills and going after the big bucks. I learned much from him as he preached time and time again to the congregation of which I was a member. His sons and I hunt together now, and I can see his legacy in them.

The thought of the new heavenly height he has reached as a redeemed child of God makes me wish I could ask him that question just once more. This time, however, I'd do it with no sarcasm whatsoever. Instead, I'd say it with a sincere longing... "How's the weather up there?"

20

The "All Day-er"

STEVE

A great day of hunting for me is when I have the time to get in a deer stand before dawn and not leave it until after the sun goes down. It was during one of those memorable "all day-ers" that I had a soul-stirring encounter with a Buckeye buck.

Several years ago I joined a group of men for an October white-tail bow hunt at the Tar Hollow State Forest in south-central Ohio. It was a highly anticipated hunt that spanned only Saturday and Sunday, and unfortunately, due to my speaking schedule, I could be there only on Saturday.

As we arrived from surrounding states on Friday, it was a total joy to meet other hunters for the first time. It was as though we couldn't talk fast enough as we shared our stories, compared equipment, and strategized about the weekend.

Besides the camo-camaraderie we enjoyed, there was another reason for the collective hunting adrenalin coursing through the veins of the nonresident participants. We were all wired and raring to hit the woods because of the reports we got from the locals who had previously hunted the thousands of acres of public land. They told us of sightings of bucks that lived up to Ohio's reputation for being the home of some heavy-antlered beasts.

Their talk of plentiful mast, the endless crop fields, and the bone-building minerals that saturated the Buckeye soil made the out-of-staters like me feel envious of the quality of bucks we might have a chance to see and maybe take. I started to wonder if picking up and moving our family to Ohio might be a smart thing to do.

I had never hunted the territory and had only one day to do it, so during dinner on Friday evening I asked one of the Ohio hunters if he would recommend an area for me to stake out. He graciously offered to escort me to a spot he had been to before and said it held great promise for some action. He was right.

Breakfast on Saturday morning was tasty but quick, and then I headed out with the local hunter who drove me to a trailhead at the base of a tall hill. In the overhead cab light, he showed me a map of the area and pointed out the ridge he thought would be a good place to put my stand. Then he asked me what time I wanted him to pick me up for lunch. My response didn't surprise him.

"Well, there's no need for that. At breakfast I grabbed a couple of granola bars, made a peanut butter sandwich, and put a couple of apples and two bottles of water in my pack. I'm here for an all day-er. I'll see you after sunset. If I get into something this morning, I'll just walk the mile back to the lodge to get some help."

My new friend smiled, pronounced a blessing on my day, and drove off into the dark. As his red taillights disappeared around the bend, I turned on my flashlight and headed up the unfamiliar hill.

The lay of the land was just as the map described. I followed an ascending trail for about three hundred yards and turned right. The leaves were moist from the overnight weather, and walking was quiet as I covered another two hundred yards and then headed uphill again. It was at that spot that I decided not to go any higher.

By then, the sky was light enough for me see my surroundings a little better, and I noticed that the woods looked very deer-ish. I looked down at the ground and saw that I was standing near a well-used trail, and I also found some fresh droppings. My one-day guide had told me that the deer normally fed low in a field below my position and tended to bed high. It seemed logical to me that I was in a place where I could possibly get some passersby, and I wouldn't be in a total sweat to start the day. Feeling good about the location, I chose a tree for my climber, quietly slid it off my back, attached it, and worked my stand up the trunk to about sixteen feet high.

By the time I was settled in, the morning light had filled the woods enough to see clearly in all directions. I was twelve yards away from the deer trail I had discovered. I felt very confident about my setup.

The anticipation I was enjoying kept me busy with nonstop visual scanning of the area. The leaves on the ground appeared a little dark, which meant they were probably still soft, and I might not hear the deer until they were very close. My guess was accurate.

Feeling a little thirsty after the morning effort, I quietly dug for one of the water bottles in my pack. I didn't realize a four-legged pedestrian was coming up the dirt street he had made on the hill. When I lifted my eyes, there he was. I nearly dropped the bottle when I saw him. The width of his rack was well beyond his ears, and I instantly calculated his weight to be at least 180 pounds. I was staring at a truly magnificent Buckeye buck. The problem was, he was staring in my direction. I couldn't move.

I had chosen a tree on the downwind side of the trail, so I was sure he didn't smell me. I thought, *But what about my movement?* I wasn't sure how much motion he had detected through the foliage between us, but it didn't appear to be enough to make him bolt and run.

The buck studied my form for about twenty seconds and then headed up the hill in a steady, relaxed walk. The encounter happened without me getting busted, but that's all it was—an encounter, and a very brief one at that. I didn't even have a chance to put a grip on the bow handle. I couldn't believe it. I had blown a great chance to fill a costly Ohio tag!

As I sat there licking my wounds, I wondered if the buck had a rival that might take the same trail. For the next half hour I didn't lower my eyes for more than a few seconds at a time. I didn't want to miss another opportunity. After a full hour, my arrow was still nocked to the string of my bow, which rested on the front rail of my climber. Then I felt a glimmer of hope as I thought about the situation.

That buck walked by me not long after daylight, and now he's lying down somewhere up there on the hill. If no one or nothing disturbs him, he could very well come right back down the trail by me about thirty minutes before dark. I'm gonna enjoy this all day-er and just look forward to him coming back. And that's what I did.

Of course, I was hoping the buck's chief rival or his older brother would come wandering up the trail that morning, but it didn't happen. Noon came, and I quietly dug through my daypack for lunch. Peanut butter and jam on white bread never tasted as good.

With lunchtime over, the minutes crawled on into the early afternoon hours, but the slow movement of the clock hands was fine with me. I cherish every second in the woods, and I'm never bored while hunting. I took the opportunity to retrieve my book of Proverbs from my pack. After reading a verse I'd look up, look around, and think about what I had just read. As I did, I couldn't help but notice how quiet the world was on that Ohio hillside. The only sounds I heard were the rustling of the leaves above me, a few birds singing to each other, and the occasional scamper of a squirrel across the leaves that had finally dried. The near silence was a sweet reward of an all-day sit.

I stood a few times to stretch and loosen my muscles, all the while keeping an eye out for deer that may have decided not to nap. At four o'clock I stood and stretched one last time for a simple and important reason. The buck I was waiting for was probably getting hungry enough to start heading to the dining room below me. If I stood again, it would be for only one reason—to get my string to full draw.

I knew that the legal shooting light would go out in the eastern time zone around six thirty, and by five thirty I was wired tighter than a brand-new barbwire fence. I couldn't wait to see if the same buck would show up again. And sure enough, he did!

This time I saw him about eighty yards up the hill, slowly descending and browsing as he came. I had seen him in plenty of time to get to my feet and attach my release to the string on the bow. If he continued the course of his decent, I had about five minutes until launch time. I wanted to shake all over but fought to control it.

My plan was to avoid moving a muscle or even blinking until he descended to about eye-level with me. It was an unwanted but unavoidable feature of the set up. I had dealt with it before, and I thought, *It won't be a problem as long as the wind stays in my favor. Oh—the wind! I forgot!*

I turned my face toward the trail to see if I could feel what the wind was doing, and my heart sank when I realized it wasn't doing what it was supposed to do. Normally it rises in the morning and falls at night. But not on this day. I could feel a breeze heading up the trail. So did the buck.

At about forty yards from my stand, he suddenly stopped and raised his head abruptly. He was in range but facing me straight on—not offering the broadside shot I needed. I could tell he had gotten a signal from his nose that something wasn't right in his world.

I wish I could say my scent suppression system worked and he continued walking down the hill, but unfortunately, that didn't happen. I was crushed to see the buck wheel around and run, with his tail raised, back up the trail and out of sight. I could hear him crashing through the leaves as he escaped my intention to take him back to the lodge with me in the bed of a truck. In an instant, ten hours of sitting patiently, quietly, and willingly in a tree stand were lost. It was as if the hand of fate had taken an eraser and wiped the words "you're the man" off the blackboard of my ego.

The commotion the buck had created around me made it certain that the hunt was done. I faced the disappointment, dismounted, and headed back down to where I had been dropped off that morning. I can't describe how much I wished I could have announced to the fellow who came to pick me up that I had a trophy Buckeye beast to check in. Instead, I was empty-handed—but not totally. I did have one good thing to take home with me.

During that Saturday, after the buck made his very brief morning appearance and then wandered out of sight, several times I stared up the hill where he had gone and whispered, "I'm looking forward to you coming back." Eventually, I realized the same words could be said to Jesus, who has promised to come again to earth someday in glory and in mighty triumph over all things evil.

Especially now, in the midst of such chaotic times, I often look heavenward and say, "I'm looking forward to You coming back!" Each time I do, I'm encouraged in my soul to watch faithfully for His return.

What a great trophy to bring home from an all day-er in Ohio.

I'M LOOKING FORWARD TO YOU COMING BACK

I took a look in the book, and on the very last page
Right there, I saw a prayer that John prayed
When he heard the words that You said to him
"Very soon I'll come again!"
Let it be, amen!

I'm looking forward to You coming back
When I see Your face, Lord, I'm gonna be glad
You know I'm grateful for the life down here I've had
But I'm looking forward to You coming back

Ol' John has been gone for a long time
But his prayer is still there in this heart of mine
When Jesus left, He didn't forget about that promise He made
To the ones who wait
Who are longing for that day

Yes, I'm looking forward to You coming back
When I see Your face, Lord, I'm gonna be glad
You know I'm grateful for the life down here I've had
But I'm looking forward to You coming back[8]

> Surely I come quickly. Amen. Even so, come, Lord Jesus
> (Revelation 22:20 KJV).

21

Left but Not Lost

DON

When pastors come across a really good sermon illustration they've never heard, they'll often say, "Oh! Now, that'll preach!" That's exactly what I said to a friend when I heard him tell about something that happened to him when he was deer hunting.

If hunters competed to see how much gear they could put in a backpack, Rick would definitely win the prize. He always carried extra ammo, food, water, a thermos of coffee, a flashlight, weather protection gear, a knife, a saw, a rope, skunk scent, acorn attractant, a cell phone, a range finder, a camera and spare batteries…just to name a few items. If my favorite outdoor store ever closes its doors, I know where I can go for supplies.

Of all the stuff Rick squeezes into his heavy pack during deer season, there's one thing he considers absolutely necessary. It's an item he says has yielded more opportunities for filling a tag than anything else in his possession. It's his old, well-tuned, highly effective grunt call. He says it's a treasure to him, and not just because he's never found one that sounds better and that is harder for bucks to resist. The call has been with him since his earliest hunting days. It's an item that connects the present with the past, and for that reason it's priceless. Thus the despair he felt one evening after the setting sun forced his exit from the woods.

As the darkness fell, and with almost surgical precision, Rick began the process of cramming impossible amounts of equipment back into his backpack. If gamblers had been nearby, they all would have given hundred-to-one odds that he would never get everything in. However, Rick was the boss of his bulging backpack, and he managed to squeeze everything into its designated spot, or so he assumed.

When he got home, he followed his usual routine of emptying and washing his thermos, cleaning his weapon, and removing the wadded-up granola bar wrappers and empty water bottle to make room for replacements. That's when he discovered that he had made an unfortunate blunder. He had left *it* behind. Out there in the dark, up a deep hollow, a long way from the road and still hanging on the limb in the tree he had occupied, was his longtime tubular friend.

Rick knew it was too late in the evening to safely retrace his steps and find the hackberry where the call hung. He couldn't believe what he'd done and knew very well he wouldn't be satisfied until he went back and got it. The idea that someone else might find it or a squirrel might decide to use it to sharpen its teeth was bothersome enough to drive him from his bed before dawn the next morning to retrieve it and still be at work on time. It took a lot of extra effort to retrieve the call, but Rick did it.

So what was it about this story that made me say, "Now, that'll preach"?

To a lot of folks, fretting over something like an old, left-behind grunt call might seem strange, and on the surface it may appear to be misplaced affection—but not to Rick. That heavy-duty plastic noisemaker not only held the precious memories of every big-antlered shooter that reacted to it by turning on its heels and heading his way—the call also held the promise of future trophy-yielding responses. That's what was attached to the tube that hung alone in the night by a lanyard on a tree limb.

Now, imagine that the grunt call had feelings. (I know this is a stretch, but go down this trail with me.) All the years of being carried and cared for had made the bond with its proud owner very deep and real. They were inseparable—that is, until one evening when it was left behind. How sad. What a long night, waiting in the darkness, wondering why it didn't go home with the hunter and asking, *Will he remember me?* But what the call didn't know was how much it was missed, how desperately hopeful its owner was that it wouldn't be stolen or harmed, and how nothing could stop him from retrieving it at first light.

If I were standing at a pastor's podium right now offering this illustration, this is the moment I would say, "Now, turn with me to John 17:9-19, and let's read an unforgettable prayer that Jesus prayed."

> I pray for them. I do not pray for the world but for those whom You have given Me, for they are Yours. And all Mine are Yours, and Yours are Mine, and I am glorified in them. Now I am no longer in the world, but these are in the world, and I come to You. Holy Father, keep through Your name those whom You have given Me, that they may be one as We are. While I was with them

in the world, I kept them in Your name. Those whom You gave Me I have kept; and none of them is lost except the son of perdition, that the Scripture might be fulfilled. But now I come to You, and these things I speak in the world, that they may have My joy fulfilled in themselves. I have given them Your word; and the world has hated them because they are not of the world, just as I am not of the world. I do not pray that You should take them out of the world, but that You should keep them from the evil one. They are not of the world, just as I am not of the world. Sanctify them by Your truth. Your word is truth. As You sent Me into the world, I also have sent them into the world. And for their sakes I sanctify Myself, that they also may be sanctified by the truth.

If this were Sunday morning, I would stop and pose a question to each one in the congregation who claimed to be a believer. "Do you, as one of God's own, ever feel like Rick's call? At times you might feel forgotten and alone in the darkness of this world, wondering if you're remembered. If so, don't ever forget how Jesus prayed about you, and by all means don't forget that at this very minute He's interceding for you. You may feel left behind at times, but you're not lost. Be encouraged in your soul as you wait for His return—and it will happen as sure as Rick went back to get his call. You can rest assured that you're much more precious to Him than you realize. He hasn't forgotten you. He proved it when He said, 'I will come again and receive you to Myself; that where I am, there you may be also'" (John 14:3).

22
The Concrete Scar

STEVE

To most of us, a superhighway is just a fast way to get from point A to point B. However, it's not that for everyone, including me. To explain what I mean, I first have to go back in time.

In the fall of 1967 I entered my senior year of high school. There were lots of clubs and teams to join, but I limited myself to just two, and for a good reason. I didn't want to load myself down with activities at school that would unduly interfere with hunting season. It was hard enough to keep academics from getting in the way.

One of the groups I joined was the Rod and Gun Club because it was filled with other guys who shared my intense love of the outdoors. I chose the second extracurricular activity because of another serious interest I had.

I played guitar and piano (both by ear) and was involved musically at every service at the church where my Dad was the pastor. I wasn't a prodigy, but I had a prodigious desire to be a musician. So when someone suggested that I try out for the school choir, I thought, *Why not! Another chance to pick and grin!* Little did I know there'd be a reason beyond music that would make me glad I signed up for the choir.

The director, Mr. Joe Head, was a fan of all types of songs, including hymns, show tunes, popular contemporary hits, and country songs. We did them all, and often Mr. Head would call on students to perform solo parts. Anne Williamson was his favorite. I had met her in the eighth grade but didn't know her well. Her alto voice was unusually rich, and Mr. Head would close his eyes and smile when she sang for him. I, too, thought her singing was extraordinary, but as lovely it was, it wasn't just her voice that captured my admiration. It was also the place she called home.

The Williamsons were dairy farmers, and they milked about 60 cows daily. By the time Anne was a senior, the milking process had become automated, but it was still a lot of hard work. Twice a day, seven days a week, she and her siblings labored side by side with their parents, gathering the milk to sell to local processors. But work wasn't the only activity on the farm, especially for her two brothers.

During the fall and winter months, if the boys weren't in the barn, they were often hunting on the 400-acre Williamson farm. I gathered this intriguing detail one day in early December when Anne told me about the eleven-point buck her brother took off their property. My ears perked up when she hinted that I would be welcome to come to their farm for a hunt.

I immediately bypassed such niceties as "How kind of you to offer," or "Thanks, I'll keep your dad's farm in mind" and went straight to the first question that came to mind. I asked if she thought her brother might put me in the stand where he bagged the monster buck.

That was bold, and her answer was a cautious yes. We agreed that I would go to their farm the following Saturday. That day during choir rehearsal, I sang a little louder and smiled bigger. I couldn't wait for the weekend to come. Anne also was happy, but for a reason I didn't know. I had responded to her on-the-spot invitation exactly the way she had hoped. Why? Because she had a crush on me! Her tactic was well timed, perfectly executed, and wisely concealed behind an eleven-point buck.

The short version of the rest of the story is that I did indeed go to the farm the next Saturday. I showed up at Anne's front door nearly two hours before sunrise and surprised the family, especially her dad. He partially opened their heavy wooden door and saw someone standing there with a rifle on the other side of the foggy glass storm door, which he didn't open. Who could blame him?

With obvious concern, he asked me why I was there. I told him Anne had invited me to their farm to hunt and that her brother would take me to his stand. Her dad told me to wait, closed the wooden door, and left me standing on the front porch in the very frigid cold. Smart man.

A few minutes later Anne's brother opened the door and was putting on his heavy coat as he walked by and simply nodded for me to follow him. I assumed he was quiet by nature but didn't know there was another reason for his silence. His vocally talented sister had not warned him about my visit.

I followed behind the family truck as he led me up the hollow. He pulled off, and I parked behind him. Without saying much, he guided me up a long hill to his special hand-built stand and waited until I climbed in. Then he left me there in the coal-black darkness and subfreezing temperature to wait nearly an hour before the sun came up. I seriously thought I wouldn't make it to daylight alive. I made it, but not without a lot of shivering.

I didn't see any deer that morning. The only thing I saw was another hunter who wandered through and messed up my hunt. I fought the urge to touch off a couple of rounds at his feet and managed to let him go unharmed. Then my cheap wristwatch froze, and I had no way to know what time it was. I panicked at the thought of not getting my dad's car back to the house in time for him to drive it to work that afternoon, so I left the hollow in a hurry, not knowing I would generate the ire of Mrs. Williamson, who made a lunch for me that I didn't stop to eat. Oh well.

Though the morning turned out to be a bust in terms of getting a big deer, and even though I garnered the disfavor of Mom Williamson due to my abrupt and rude departure, one wonderful and lasting thing did come of the hunt. Anne had figured out that the way to a man's heart is through his tree stand. From that Saturday on I would not forget her. In fact, as time progressed, love began to blossom in my heart for her. We started dating in 1974 and married in the spring of 1975.

Today, Anne is known as Annie. Her name was altered because the music group we were in during the mid-1970s had another member named Anne. Annie is the most cherished "dear" I took off the Williamson farm! To say the least, for that reason alone, her family's 400 acres hold a very special place in my heart.

Through the years, I was privileged to hunt the other kind of deer on her family property, and I enjoyed some unforgettable encounters, including one with the "four thirty buck." I refer to it that way because I pulled the trigger at precisely that time after following Mr. Williamson's advice. I had hunted four mornings and three evenings on another part of the farm and had only one evening left to try. He had watched the deer's ritual and suggested I be in a certain spot on the hill behind their house when it came through. The buck ended up in my freezer!

I made an even more precious hunting memory on the farm. I was sitting beside our ten-year-old son when he bagged his first critter as a hunter. With a single-shot .410 shotgun, he got a plump gray squirrel that he took to his Grandma Williamson for her to fry. She added some of her awesome gravy and biscuits to the mix, and the scrumptious wild-game meal capped a day that will forever be etched on my heart.

Then there were the rabbit hunts on the farm that were highlights of our annual Christmas visits. Barking beagles, the flashes of fur darting through the underbrush, the smell of expended shotgun shells, the hilarious verbal exchanges with Annie's brothers as we hunted...all these and more are embedded in my soul.

Many other great memories of the family property fill several pages of my life's story. I looked forward to making many more entries in the years that would follow, but then came some news I didn't want to hear. The West Virginia highway department planned to build an interstate through the Williamson farm. My heart sank, and I quietly hoped that it was just a rumor or that somehow the project would get hung up in legal battles with landowners and county leaders. But instead, the State fired up the bulldozers and broke ground.

The Williamson farm, located nine miles from the starting point of construction, didn't feel the rumble of the huge Caterpillars and logging trucks right away. I was able to enjoy hunting on the land until the passing of Annie's parents. After they were gone, the land was disbursed among the siblings, and much of it was sold to other families. The home place became a rental, occupied by folks I didn't know. Though there were strangers moving onto the land, in my mind it was still the Williamson farm. And even though it's been years since I've hunted there, I still consider it dear to my heart.

Amazingly, when the first section of the four-lane highway was completed, it stopped about three-quarters of a mile from the hill directly behind the house where Annie had lived. I was relieved to think that maybe the State had decided to call it quits. Perhaps the grounds and the memories I had made there would remain undisturbed after all.

But during a recent drive back to the area, I discovered that the dozers were no longer silent. Driving down the old two-lane highway I had taken years earlier on that first morning, I turned right onto Nine Mile Road, which led to the farm. I just wanted to take a drive down memory lane and see the place. As I drove up the beautiful, narrow, winding blacktop road toward the Williamson house, a warm feeling washed over me. Our kids called it the Peaceful Lane when they were youngsters.

When I rounded the familiar final bend before reaching the gravel driveway I had turned into many times, I could see the house where my sweet wife was raised. It still looked inviting as it sat nestled in the trees at the foot of the hill. However, behind the white brick home was a sight that made me very sad.

At the top of the hill nearby was a wide gap in the tree line. The tall, old timber had been recently cleared down to the raw dirt. I immediately knew what had happened, and I can't explain how much I wished my eyes were playing tricks on me. The four-lane highway had arrived.

I continued on up the hollow past the home place, and a few hundred yards beyond the next bend I saw two sets of seven massive pylons rising up out of the ground. They were there to support the parallel bridges that would cross over Nine Mile Road. There was no stopping the progress. I didn't want to face it, but I knew that in time the once pristine property where so many great memories had been made would be marred by pavement.

I took a few pictures of the construction with my phone and then turned around and slowly drove back toward the main highway. As I once again passed the gravel driveway that led to the Williamson house, I said a silent farewell to the property. It was painful to think that the only way I'd ever hunt the farm again would be in the quiet of remembrance.

Now you know why I see our nation's network of multilane highways through different eyes today. I don't resent their existence. In fact, I'm grateful for the openness and convenience our big roads offer. But as I drive along and enjoy the beautiful countryside scenery, I'm aware that somewhere nearby there's a farmer, a family, and very likely a hunter who wishes their neck of the woods had never been cut by the knife of progress. Though time may heal the wound, there will always be a concrete scar to remind them of the pain of change.

THIS CONCRETE SCAR

I feel the rhythm of the highway
Making music as I ride
I see the fields beyond the shoulders
Woods and hills and valleys wide

As I go from here to yonder
On this ribbon made of stone
I can't forget the ground beneath me
Could well have been somebody's home

The roar of diesels in their timber
Calling for their sacrifice
Chains of razor, blades of iron
Cut their memories like a knife

And like the marks that tell love's story
On the Savior's hands and feet
This concrete scar on which I travel
Tells of what they gave for me[9]

23
The Abandoned Fawn

DON

Tony loves the woodlands and the silence and serenity they offer. He cherishes his quiet times with God, especially when he's hunting. While sitting in a stand one morning he saw a lone fawn wander into a field about an hour after sunrise. It had apparently gotten separated from the herd. Tony's heart melted with the sight, and he whispered as if the fawn could hear what he said. "Abandoned—I know how you feel, little buddy."

As a child, Tony always wanted to miss the first day of school. It wasn't because he didn't like the classroom or that he didn't want to take part in the fun of the first day. There was another reason he didn't care for it. He knew everybody would be asked to introduce themselves, share things about their family, and play word games that would help them remember their fellow classmates' names. Each student would learn where all the other kids lived, how long they had lived there, what their parents' names were, and what their parents did for a living. Tony dreaded talking about these details.

Telling the kids about his mother or her job at the local shirt factory was not the problem. Lots of moms worked there since it was the area's biggest industry. Tony's Kentucky hometown thrived on the fabric industry. The people were better off monetarily because of the big trucks hauling shirts, socks, and jeans from the plant to the rest of the country. He was proud of the fact that his mother was a part of it all. So talking about her on the first day was easy.

It was his dad that he preferred not to discuss.

Tony knew that if he couldn't act sick enough, cough loud enough, or persuade his mom that his head hurt bad enough, he'd be thrown once again into the lion's den of questions that his teacher would ask. "What's your father's name?" "What does he do?"

Tony's attempt to feign sickness failed, and he was off to school. Sure enough, those questions were asked. He didn't respond immediately. He had to let a few seconds go by as he reached down as deep as he could for courage. Then he held up his head and gave the dreaded reply.

"I don't know. I don't know who he is, and I don't know what he does."

The answer brought a dramatic moment of quiet in the room. As the teacher processed her regret for asking the question, Tony had to deal with wondering if his answer had instantly placed him in a box, separated from everyone else. Was he now *different*? Tony hated that first day of school!

People say that time heals all hurts. Maybe so, but the healing is not always complete, and it wasn't in Tony's case. As he grew older, the hidden residue of pain seemed to fester. To add to the hurt, over the years he began to piece together the story of his life, how the relationship between his parents was short lived, and how marriage was never a part of their experience. He also discovered that he wasn't the only one living in pain all those years. His mom was hurting as well. Tony began to realize that she blamed herself for the brokenness in their lives, and the guilt haunted her heart every day.

Perhaps to fight the gnawing loneliness he felt or simply to get out of his house, when Tony entered his teenage years he began attending a local church. His decision to go sit in a pew turned out to be a very good thing. It was at church where he noticed that people referred to God as their Father. It sounded strange to him. And when the pastor talked about the heavenly Father caring deeply about each and every person, no matter who, what, or where they were, Tony silently wondered, *If the heavenly Father loved everyone so much, why am I fatherless? Why do I have to deal with this disappointment of not having a father? Why do I have to feel so helpless and alone?*

Normally, a kid with questions like these might resist and reject the idea that God is a loving Father. However, Tony became more and more intrigued with the Scriptures about this Father, and he began to attend church regularly. One Sunday morning, he heard an amazing story about God the Father sending His Son to die so that others could live. He also learned that like himself, Jesus was an only Son.

For the first time, Tony began to realize that all along, God, the heavenly Father, had shown His love through his mom, his grandpa, his grandma, and others who were placed in his life to care for him from his youth to the present day. Feeling grateful for how he had been so loved, and having a longing to know his Father in heaven, he responded to an invitation to commit his life to Christ.

Tony was never the same. He knew in his heart and soul that he belonged to a spiritual family and had a real Father. He had never felt such joy in all his years.

Tony began working with youth groups, church programs, and Bible schools. He was asked to teach, to lead worship, and even to speak on Sunday morning. It wasn't long until he realized that the ministry was his calling, his purpose in life.

One night as he sat alone, pondering the new experience he was living, Tony made a lifelong commitment. He wanted to preach the gospel. He wanted to be the one to stand and tell the world the great news that the heavenly Father loved them. Soon after that he was ordained and placed into the work of ministry while attending a Bible college. At the very tender age of eighteen he was offered the position of leading his first church as pastor. He accepted the position and was one of the youngest ever to do so in the area.

One day, as Tony thought about the many people who were hearing the gospel through his ministry, he wondered about his dad. His heart began to burn with the desire to find his earthly father and share the plan of salvation with him. Even though his dad had not fulfilled his obligation to him, Tony didn't want him to miss out on a relationship with God and an eternal home in heaven.

Time passed, Tony's ministry flourished, and he moved several times over the next dozen years. Although his life took many turns and covered many roads, he never stopped praying, *Heavenly Father, I ask that somehow, somewhere, You will help me to tell my dad about You.*

On a weekday day like every other weekday at the church, Tony sat in his study, faithfully planning and preparing to deliver another message the following Sunday. As he worked extra hard to complete his preparation before leaving the office to go visit some folks in the hospital, the phone rang.

"Hello?"

An unfamiliar voice at the other end of the line asked, "Is this Tony?"

"Yes, it is."

"Tony, this is your dad."

There was total silence. The intensity of Tony's emotions in that moment was indescribable. The list of questions he had always wanted to ask his dad instantly appeared in his mind, but at the top was the one Tony had prayed about for twelve years.

After a few words of greeting, he said, "Dad…"

Tony stopped. For the first time in his life, he spoke *that* word to another man. It felt odd, but it also felt really good. With a tone of respect in his voice, he boldly continued.

"Dad…do you know Christ as your Savior?"

There was not a moment of silence or hesitation on the other end of the line. "Yes, Tony, I accepted Christ a short time ago, and that's when I began my search for you. I desperately wanted to find you and ask for your forgiveness."

Tony could have been knocked over with a feather when he heard his father's testimony. Tears of joy flowed as he congratulated his dad. They talked for several minutes and then scheduled a time to meet. When the day finally came to make the drive to the most meaningful rendezvous of his lifetime, the many miles were filled with imagining what it was going to be like.

Meeting his father turned out to be all that Tony expected—more tears, bear hugs, answered questions, and even a heartbroken father's sincere, face-to-face apology. The experience was unforgettable to say the least.

While driving home the next day, Tony repeatedly expressed his deepest thanks to God for allowing him such a life-changing encounter—one for which he had so diligently prayed. He could never have known that only four weeks later, he would get the phone call telling him that his father had died. With all the reverence for his sovereign God that he could muster, he cried out to Him, "Why so soon?"

It wasn't easy, but Tony finally accepted the reality that his relationship with his dad, though brief, was an answer to prayer. He chose to be thankful for the fact that God had allowed him to meet his dad on this side of heaven, and he took great comfort in knowing that the next time they would embrace would be at a forever meeting.

Tony continued watching the lone fawn that reminded him of his past. Then the small herd it belonged to appeared at the edge of the field. There seemed to be a dance in the young deer's steps as he rejoined the group. Once again, as if the fawn could hear him, Tony smiled and said, "How relieved you must be. I know how you feel!"

Dear heavenly Father, please speak to the lonely, the fatherless ones at this moment and let them know You are willing and able to fill the void they feel in their hearts. And if a father who has abandoned a little one is reading these words right now, I pray that You will give him courage to yield his life to You and then find the desire to reconnect with that abandoned one. I ask this to the glory of Your only begotten Son. In His name, amen.

GOING BACK

What I find in going back
Chasing memories down the track
The little boy sitting in that pew
Playing with the songbooks in the rack
Dreaming, "I'll lasso that big moon
Or kill a giant in the lagoon"

After years of living I face the fact
That I'm still longing to go back
To have the choice to live again
To run from here and go back to then
To know back there what now I see
Though all alone He was with me
Thru all the years to know I had
The God of heaven as my best dad[10]

24

The Wise Old Hunter

STEVE

One of the most enjoyable things I've seen when I travel and speak at wild-game dinner events is a camo-clad granddad with his camo-wearing grandson. When I see a young boy with an older gentleman, I like to ask, "Who's this with you?" When the answer confirms my assumption that it's a grandpa with a grandson, I often probe a little further about why they came together to such an event. Very often I've learned some interesting dynamics about their relationships.

Some of the boys are with their gramps because their dad was working and simply couldn't be there. Some accompany their grandpa because the dad is absent due to an unfortunate circumstance such as separation, divorce, or death. In some cases, the grandpa is the only one in the family who loves to hunt, and he introduced his grandson to the outdoors. Whatever the reason they attended the event together, it's always a delight to see a grandfather invest time, energy, and resources in his children's children.

Someone once said that granddads are there to help their grand-kids get into the mischief they haven't thought of yet. That's a sober-ing thought, and my grandkids' parents would say there's a lot of truth in it. (Maybe the whoopee cushion I bought for them is to blame). The real truth is that in addition to being a source of fun for grandkids, grandparents can draw from their wealth of experience to teach youngsters some helpful lessons that will benefit them in profound ways.

For example, while a grandfather shows a grandson how to make a slingshot from a fallen oak limb, some leather from an old shoe tongue, and strips of rubber from a discarded inner tube, he also can teach the boy that some things may seem worthless but are redeemable and useful. Here's another example of how granddads can be life changers as they plant eternal truths in the soil of grand-children's hearts.

GOD'S GONNA KEEP YOU IN HIS SIGHTS

He was twelve years old sittin' with his grandpa
Underneath that big oak tree way up in the hollow
Watching for whitetail in that November sun
Holdin' on tight to that Winchester gun

They started talkin' and kept it to a whisper
About beagles and baseball and puttin' up with sisters
Then like a wise old hunter his grandpa said
"As long you live, boy, don't you forget…

"God's gonna keep you in His sights
He'll be lookin' out for you, you're precious in His eyes
Wherever you go on the trail of this life, you'll be all right
'Cause God's gonna keep you in His sights"

Year after year they were in those hills together
Makin' those memories, the kind that last forever
Then came the season when the world went to war
The boy was just nineteen when he landed on that shore

And in that moment way down in his soul
He could hear his grandpa's voice comin' from that hollow
Sayin'

"God's gonna keep you in His sights
He'll be lookin' out for you, you're precious in His eyes
Wherever you go on the trail of this life, you'll be all right
'Cause God's gonna keep you in His sights"[11]

I'm a grandfather, and I'm very aware that I have influence. You do too if you're a granddad. I pray for both of us, that God will help us be good and worthy examples to our grandsons and granddaughters. To help me accomplish that goal, I take inspiration from the well-known Gospel story about the woman caught in the act of adultery. It reminds me of how much influence my example can have. Maybe it will help you too.

In the story, Jesus challenges those who are about to stone the adulteress to death by saying, "He who is without sin among you, let him be the first to throw a stone at her." Then the passage says,

"When they heard it, they began to go out one by one, beginning with the older ones " (John 8:7,9 NASB).

When I read the story, it occurred to me that the younger men in the crowd probably wouldn't have dropped their stones and walked away if the older ones hadn't done so first. That detail in the scene is a serious heads-up for me. My grandkids notice what I say, what I do, how I act, and where I go. It's true for you and yours too. For their sake, I pray that God will help us be wise old hunters and not squander our unique opportunity to bless our children's children by living a life worth imitating.

> Be imitators of me, as I am of Christ (1 Corinthians 11:1 ESV).

25
The Hunt Is Over

DON

It's midafternoon late in the fall, and the sun has started its journey to its nightly hiding place behind the western wall of timber. Shadows become slightly longer as I enjoy waiting for an elusive deer that I affectionately refer to as the big cottontail. So far it's been a great season, just like seasons past, except for one thing.

I've noticed that just as the leaves change after the summer ends, things have been changing in my body now that I'm beyond the summer of my life. The creaks I've been hearing recently while climbing into my stand are not from loose metal but from loose joints and brittle bones.

I'm wise enough to know that these days, in order for the muscles of my aging frame to move me twenty feet up into my tree stand, I have to force my mind to believe I'm twenty-five again. But after I sit down, it's not long until the truth returns and I feel the aftermath of the effort it took to climb in. As my back moans with its aching, I silently admit it to myself, *Yes, I'm in the autumn of life.*

Lately I've been spending more time assessing where I am on the graph of time. I ask myself the same questions. *How many more seasons do I have? How many more trips will God give me to this pulpit above the congregation of animals that attend this woodland temple? If I am "just a vapor that appears for a little while and then vanishes away"* (James 4:14 NASB), *how much more time will I hang around?* Only God knows the answers.

It's November, and because most of the leaves have fallen, the view from where I sit in the woods extends down into the hollow below me. I don't need binoculars to see the old homemade stand that was once some other hunter's personal perch. It was skillfully built and well used but eventually left behind by a sportsman who might have found a better spot or maybe whose seasons have forever ended. Who knows?

Whatever the story was in regard to the unused stand, I look on it with reverence and admiration, wishing I could hear every detail of the hunting tales it could tell. Some completely true, some with the truth a bit stretched, and maybe a few beyond belief. I imagine the stand was ascended many times by its builder as well as by hunters who wandered through (or were even trespassing) and, recognizing its great location, took the liberty to use it. I feel certain it had lots of stories to tell, but the book they're recorded in was closed by the hands of time and can't be reopened.

My mind returns to the hunt, and only God and I know how much I wish this day could last forever. How sweet are nature's gifts—a slight breeze, abundant acorns, a place to rest for a while from life's daily grind, and the constant anticipation of possibly adding an entry into the Pope and Young record book. The mere thought makes me grip the bow handle a little tighter. I can almost see myself dragging out a twelve pointer.

I think to myself, *If I don't tag the big one today, there is always tomorrow.* But then the cold mist of reality moves into the woods around me and chills my heart. Something or someone whispers, *Maybe you won't get another tomorrow. Maybe you have just today, just this minute, this moment, this breath. Don't forget, the night will come when no man can hunt.*

This brief but unforgettable encounter with the truth about the brevity of my days brings more emotion than I care to work through at the moment, so I refocus on the hunt and coach myself. *Don't move too quickly. Don't turn too fast or even breathe hard. He may be a mere fifty yards away, through that brush, behind that clump of trees, around the bend.*

I've just got to hang on, be patient, be still. I wait and watch, but no deer stroll by this evening. And then, as the sun begins to yield to a rising moon, I take a final peek down the hollow at the old stand. I'm not sure, but I think I spot an old man on his feet in that rotten old platform.

No, a closer look reveals that it's only a branch waving on the other side of its dilapidated foundation. Then I remember how sundown in the woods can darken every stump, sapling, and rock, mysteriously making things appear to change shape.

I slowly and carefully tie my rope to my weapon and lower it to the ground. I stand to prepare for my descent and feel stiff from sitting motionless for so long. My muscles might be weak, but my hope for success following tomorrow's sunrise is still strong.

As the day of hunting disappears into the past, the deep darkness falls quickly around me. With it comes the strange feeling that I'm a million miles from anything familiar, even though I know the property like the back of my hand. I begin my walk out of the back field toward the lights of home, and thoughts of the warmth waiting for me make me walk faster. I look forward to seeing the one who knows I'll have another story to tell when I arrive, one she really doesn't care to hear. She'll listen anyway and pretend she's enthralled by it. It's her act of love. It will be great just to have her understanding ear with that first cup of dinner coffee.

Most likely tonight we will share a meal, watch TV for a while, retire to bed, and read and pray together. Then I'll rest my "autumn season" body with a night of healing sleep. I'll set the clock, and when it wakes me I'll rise to get ready for another hunt—at least that's my plan. Then I remember a haunting reality.

It's not easy to face the truth that someday I won't be putting on my hi-top, rubber-bottomed boots or my fleece-lined, camo coat. I won't throw my backpack over my shoulders and pick up my gun to head to the woods. Instead, I'll be that hunter who abandoned his stand and left it for a younger man to find and imagine who the old guy was that once used it. I know it's inevitable that I too will someday walk into the fields of eternity. For that reason I want to be careful to cherish every walk through the early morning dew, every quiet and restful midday vigil, and every return to my beloved. I want to do these things until I hear God say, "Well done, My child, the hunt is over."

> LORD, make me to know my end
> And what is the extent of my days;
> Let me know how transient I am (Psalm 39:4 NASB).

THE HUNT IS OVER

At early morn' I slowly rise to go and face the beast,
I'll race against the new sun rising in the east,

I'll one last time look slowly back to view my earthly home,
And to the darkened room on the second floor,
Where my lover sleeps alone.
And then I'll make that final turn that leads to my best place
Where many times, down thru the years, I've made my
    hunting chase.
I'll slowly place my bow or gun upon earth's dew-drenched clover,
And listen close till evening says, "My child, the hunt is over."[12]

For more information about Steve Chapman's books, music, and speaking schedule, visit
www.steveandanniechapman.com

To contact Don Hicks about resources and speaking, visit
www.realmomentsoftruth.com

Notes

1. Don Hicks, "The Hurting Path," © 2012 by Don Hicks.
2. Steve Chapman, "We're Gonna Talk About Jesus," © 2014 by Times & Seasons Music.
3. Don Hicks, "Master of the Morning," © 2012 by Don Hicks.
4. Steve Chapman and Lindsey Williams, "You Just Never Know" © 2014 by Times & Seasons Music / Really Big Bison Music.
5. Steve Chapman, "Back to the Blood," © 2015 by Times & Seasons Music.
6. Don Hicks, "What I Saw," © 2012 by Don Hicks.
7. Steve Chapman and Annie Chapman, "He's Not There," © 2016 by Times & Seasons Music.
8. Steve Chapman, Annie Chapman, and Shane Brown, "I'm Looking Forward to You Coming Back," © 2014 by Times & Seasons Music / Shane Brown Music.
9. Steve Chapman, "The Concrete Scar," © 2016 by Steve Chapman.
10. Don Hicks, "Going Back," © 2012 by Don Hicks.
11. Steve Chapman, "God's Gonna Keep You in His Sights," © 2016 by Times & Seasons Music.
12. Don Hicks, "The Hunt Is Over," © 2011 by Don Hicks.

More Great Harvest House Books for Sportsmen

BY STEVE CHAPMAN

Another Look at Life from a Deer Stand

A Look at Life from a Deer Stand Devotional

A Look at Life from the Riverbank

365 Things Every Hunter Should Know

Great Hunting Stories

The Hunter's Cookbook

The Hunter's Devotional

My Dream Hunt in Alaska

One-Minute Prayers for Hunters

A Sportsman's Call

Stories from the Deer Stand

The Tales Hunters Tell

With Dad on a Deer Stand

To learn more about Harvest House books and
to read sample chapters, visit our website:

www.harvesthousepublishers.com

HARVEST HOUSE PUBLISHERS
EUGENE, OREGON